SEASONS
on the Farm

A Celebration of
Country Life Through the Year

Amy Glaser, Editor

Voyageur Press

First published in 2007 by Voyageur Press, an imprint of MBI Publishing Company LLC, Galtier Plaza, Suite 200, 380 Jackson Street, St. Paul, MN 55101 USA

Copyright © 2007 by MBI Publishing Company

Voyageur Press titles are also available at discounts in bulk quantity for industrial or sales-promotional use. For details write to Special Sales Manager at MBI Publishing Company, Galtier Plaza, Suite 200, 380 Jackson Street, St. Paul, MN 55101 USA.

To find out more about our books, join us online at www.voyageurpress.com.

Editor: Amy Glaser
Designer: Sara Holle

Printed in China

Library of Congress Cataloging-in-Publication Data

Seasons on the farm : a celebration of country life through the year / Amy Glaser, editor.
    p. cm.
  ISBN-13: 978-0-7603-2776-0 (hardbound w/ jacket)
  ISBN-10: 0-7603-2776-9 (hardbound w/ jacket) 1.
Farm life. 2. Essays. I. Glaser, Amy.
S521.S457 2007
630—dc22
                                2007011536

Permissions:
"Christmas Kaleidoscope" from *Christmas Remembered* by Ben Logan. Copyright © 1997 by Ben Logan. Used by permission of the author.

"A Tough and Hardy Breed," "Winter Mornings," "Ice Skating," and "Farm Breakfasts" from *Ya, Ya! Those Were the Days: Nostalgic Tales of the Past* by Bob Becker. Copyright © 1993 by Robert Becker. Used by permission of the author.

"Frank, Pinky, and Harry" from *When Chores Were Done: Boyhood Tales* by Jerry Apps. Copyright © 1999, 2006 by Jerold W. Apps. Used by permission of the author.

"Feeding the Critters" from *How to Shovel Manure and Other Life Lessons for the Country Woman* by Gwen Petersen. Copyright © 1976, 2007 by Gwen Petersen. Used by permission of the author.

Credits:
On the cover: The entire family (including a variety of animals) comes out to see the new tractor that Father brought home in this photo from a 1952 International Harvester calendar. Son tests out the seat while Mother and Daughter look on.

On the frontispiece: The sun sets over a barn on Pine Lake, just north of Somerset, Wisconsin. *Lee Klancher*

Title page: A father and son wave to a mother as they head to the house after their nightly chores in this illustration that appeared in an International Harvester calendar from 1952.

Contents page: There's nothing like a huge slice of homegrown watermelon on a hot summer day. This cherubic grin was featured on the cover of *Farmer's Wife* magazine.

Acknowledgments page: An aerial photograph of the Kenneth and Shirley Glaser dairy farm, located in rural Ridgeland, Wisconsin, circa 1972. *Courtesy of Kenneth and Shirley Glaser*

On the back cover (top): A tractor rambles past a freshly plowed field on a bright spring day. *Vasiliy Koval, shutterstock*
On the back cover (middle): The ice-encased barbed wire is a shining example of how brutal winter's ice and cold can be on the farm. *David S. Baker, shutterstock*
On the back cover (bottom): The county fair is an eagerly anticipated event that occurs during the summer. In this illustration from the 1952 International Harvester calendar, Mother is bringing home a coveted blue ribbon.

Acknowledgments

I would like to thank everyone who helped create this book. Roger Welsch, Robert Pripps, Michael Perry, Lee Klancher, Jerry Apps, Jessie Bylander, Carolyn Lumsden, Samantha Johnson, Philip Hasheider, Ben Logan, Gwen Petersen, and Bob Becker contributed the wonderful essays that reflect a handful of the many events that happen on a farm during the seasons that shape life in the country. Thank you to Paulette Johnson and the crew at Fox Hill Farm; Lee Klancher; David and Jean Grindle; and Kenneth and Shirley Glaser for providing photos that illustrate rural life. Many thanks go to everyone at Voyageur Press and MBI Publishing, especially to Michael Dregni for his guidance throughout the project.

Contents

In the past, windmills operated the farm's well system. Today they are primarily used as decoration and remain an icon of rural life. Pam Burley, shutterstock

INTRODUCTION

Most of the everyday duties on the farm change with the season. Considering that all aspects of the farm are deeply connected to the weather, it's no surprise the occupations of stewards on the farm are affected by the ever-changing seasons. This collection of essays highlights some of the events that occur on the farm during the year.

The farm comes to life in the spring. It's the beginning of a new growing season when all that was dormant during the winter bursts into life. Roger Welsch gives us a lesson on the first signs of spring, which can be deceiving. However, a sure sign of spring is when the sap of the maple trees starts to run. Robert Pripps educates us on the maple-sugaring process at his family farm. If you own sheep, spring is a very busy time of the year. Michael Perry tells us about growing up on a farm with sheep and his assistance during a recent lambing season on his parents' farm.

The warmth of spring soon turns into the sweltering heat of summer. When not in the field, many farmers spend their summer days at auctions obtaining more machinery for the farm. Jessie Kay Bylander regales us with the life lessons she learned while attending auctions with her father. Rural life can often be isolated, and isolation felt even more evident during the first half of the twentieth century. Jerry Apps takes us back to a time when weekend entertainment consisted of a few neighbors banding together to play music so that others could forget about their problems for a few hours by dancing them away. To many, summer on the farm means baling hay. Lee Klancher tells us how he earned his rural stripes by helping his neighbors during this annual task.

Autumn is the time for harvest. After a summer of hard work, fall is a time when life can slow down a bit. There is time to celebrate a successful growing season and harvest. Scarecrows were once just a method to scare away pests but have now become a symbol of autumn. Samantha Johnson weaves a tale of the scarecrow's practical role and its decorative, festive purpose on the farm. Autumn is also a time of reflection. Philip Hasheider's essay reflects on how fall can symbolize life and rebirth. People and lessons always remain alive in our memories. Fall is when we celebrate Thanksgiving. Harvest suppers are a rural tradition, and Carolyn Lumsden writes about this annual event that brings the community together to give thanks for all that they have received.

As the cold north wind blows in and winter envelops the farm, every duty is affected by the cold and snow. Bundling up in layers, but not too many, is the key to staying warm and preserving your appendages. Gwen Petersen gives advice on how to dress for winter chores and describes how the winter weather affects feeding the animals, especially if your husband's back is in bad shape. Bob Becker reminisces about mornings at his grandparents' farm, including the hearty breakfasts his grandmother would prepare, and ice skating at the local pond. The stark winter landscapes and dark mornings cause many to reflect on winters past. Ben Logan writes about the year's fifth season, Christmas, and spins the kaleidoscope of holiday memories.

The essays and photographs collected for this anthology were selected in the hopes that they will remind you of your own seasons on the farm and bring back memories of splashing through mud puddles in the spring, relaxing on the porch after a hot summer day, picking squash and pumpkins from the garden before the first hard frost occurs in the fall, and breathing in the crisp winter air as you brave the elements to complete your daily chores.

CHAPTER I

Spring

Listen, can you hear it? Spring's sweet cantata.
The strains of grass pushing through the snow.
The song of buds swelling on the vine.
The tender timpani of a baby robin's heart. Spring.
–Diane Frolov and Andrew Schneider
***Northern Exposure*, "Wake Up Call"**

Spring on the farm begins a new year full of life and promise. Animals that have spent the winter indoors run and kick up their heels during their first venture into the clean, fresh air. Farmers impatiently wait for the ground to solidify, so they can plant the crops for harvest in the fall. Children dig out their rubber boots and splash around in the welcoming spring rains. The drab brown grass and muddy back roads revealed by the newly melted snow are tolerably unsightly as the warming temperatures bring hope for a successful growing season.

This Farmer's Notebook from 1907 contained useful information about manuring and fertilization, as well as blank pages for recording tips or data. German Kali Works created the notebook and offered a list of free books that farmers could send for to help them on the farm.

Opposite: This old building rests on a ranch built in the 1890s in Montana. A snowstorm blanketed Harris Mountain and the foothills with white on a cool May morning.
Lee Klancher

One of the many signs of spring is the arrival of baby animals on the farm. This chestnut foal is grazing in a lush, spring field. Daniel Johnson

Signs of Spring

By Roger Welsch

Roger Welsch can best be described as a cross between Erma Bombeck and Dr. Ruth, except male and living in Nebraska with his wife and dogs. Before turning his talents to canine psychology, Roger was best known as "the fat guy in overalls" on CBS' Sunday Morning, where he offered up essays on rural and small-town life on the Plains.

Many also know him as the fat guy with the fetish for old tractors, an advocate for Native American interests, and the second-most prominent citizen of Dannebrog, Nebraska (population 352). He's also the author of numerous books of fiction and folk humor, and he writes for publications such as Successful Farming *and* Reader's Digest.

In this essay, Roger relies on his wisdom and intuition to inform us of the sure-fire signs of spring. Just when do those signs happen? Well, Rog is still working on that scientific research.

My perceptions about spring are determined almost completely by my personal and lifelong geographic orientation. I've spent most my life right here in the Middle of Nowhere, the Middle of Everywhere, smack dab in the middle of the nation—Nebraska—and all of the last thirty years smack dab in the middle of Nebraska: Howard County. I'm educated and traveled enough to have strong suspicions that what I know about spring doesn't translate to other parts of the nation or world, so you'll have to keep that in mind as you consider my confusion—starting with I don't even know when it is spring.

It doesn't help that out here in the middle of America's Steppes, the Great Plains, spring lasts about three-quarters of an hour and usually comes as a total surprise one afternoon in May, probably when I've just eaten lunch and am taking a nap. Or maybe April. Or June. That's another problem—not only is a Plains spring so short in duration you might miss it altogether, you never know when it's going to start, so if you're not keeping a sharp eye out for it, it's liable to be over before you even notice.

On the Plains (and I suspect in a lot of other places, too) you can pretty much forget about all the conventional, standard, authorized, official thresholds usually cited for the arrival of spring. March 20, the vernal (fancy word for spring) equinox, is when the day and night are of equal length and is used in almanacs and on calendars as the official celestial arrival of spring, but around here, it only means that once again I forgot my wife Linda's birthday and have roughly twelve hours to get to town and find a gift that suggests I gave a lot of time and thought to it this time. While the thing about day and night being equal and the sun rising and setting dead east and west on this day means a lot to me and the six or eight other druids in Howard County, Nebraska, for people in the city, it means only that they have to face directly into the sun both going to and coming home from work. In my days of teaching at a major university, I was dismayed and discouraged to find out how few young people today even know that the sun comes up in the east every morning, or that the point of its rising and setting moves along the horizon in a regular and cosmically profound way. My own daughter, who grew up in the rural countryside, can't even tell which direction is east or west, yet notice the sun coming up or setting there.

Moreover, while March 20 certainly comes about the time everyone is sick and tired of winter and more than ready for spring, the fact of the matter is, on March 20, we have at least four, maybe six, more weeks of wet and cold ahead of us. Our worst blizzard this year came in March, and that is anything but unusual. The perfidy of March falsely promising an imminent spring has, in fact, been noted in the folk wisdom of the rural Plains. One old settler told me that it isn't so much the long winters that make the

Piglets are an adorable sight, but they can be hard little buggers to catch. It doesn't take baby animals very long to get up to speed when it comes to outrunning farm folk! Daniel Johnson

Opposite:
Once the ground is thawed and has soaked up the snowmelt, it's time to hop on the tractor and get into the fields. There is plenty of plowing and planting ahead in the clear spring days. Daniel Johnson

trouble as it is the seventy-eight days in March. Another opined to me with painful accuracy that, "March in Nebraska is like a Model A Ford—just enough spring in it to make your ass tired."

I suspect that if we had access to psychiatric records across the nation, we might be able to judge at least the progress of winter toward spring with the increase in cases of cabin fever. They are especially common among women like Linda who are stranded on isolated farms around the rural countryside and trapped with . . . well, let's be honest about this . . . guys like me for months at a time. Maybe there is such

an index somewhere if we just knew what fancy term head doctors use for cabin fever.

There was a time when I could gauge how the year was moving along by what sports reporters were talking about on television or radio. Basketball, a winter sport, was winding up, and baseball was about to start. That was a sure sign of spring, right? The Stanley Cup hockey playoffs meant the ice was about to go off the ponds of northern climes and spring was just around the corner. Not now. Sometime around

It is a very fun day on the farm when a box full of baby chicks arrives on your doorstep. Norvia Behling

Opposite:
This Holstein cow is cleaning her newborn calf. Within minutes the calf will be up on its wobbly legs and walking around. Norvia Behling

the week that the last snows are melting, football shows up on the television screen. Football? In the spring and summer? What the heck is *that* about? And then everyone stands around scratching their heads wondering why players are falling down all around them with heat strokes. Just as football starts way too early these days, basketball goes on forever. I get the feeling that one college basketball season ends about a week before the next one begins.

Even the vaunted April showers of song, as often as not, wind up piling a few inches of sleet or snow along our fence lines. I won't take the time here to remark on the science of meteorologists, the only guys besides baseball pitchers who can make a decent living hitting the ball less than 10 percent of the time, but a common comment around here following a botched forecast is, "'Partly cloudy,' the man said last night. Well, this morning we woke up to find eight inches of 'partly cloudy' drifted up against the barn door." April showers and dancing in the streets with an umbrella morph more realistically into grabbing the weather radio and flashlight and heading for the storm cellar since any dancing that is done in gravel road country is more likely to be done by tornados.

Easter? Easter blizzards are famous around here. Besides, the way Easter jumps around on the calendar, it's even less predictable than spring. One thing is for darn sure, if you plan some sort of big family gathering like a wedding in your backyard for Easter weekend this year, you can pretty much bet winter isn't done with you yet.

I cannot for the life of me imagine who came up with the whole thing about the groundhog predicting the remaining days of winter on February 2. It may be

Farm dogs like to be where the action is on the farm. Even though they are one of the most hard-working members of the farm family, they still like to catch a ride now and then. Daniel Johnson

Opposite:
Springtime pastures are full of kids kicking up their heels in the sun. Here is an African Pygmy doe with her kid. Norvia Behling

an Indian joke. Some idiot white settler asked the experienced Native how much more winter he could expect, and the smart-aleck Indian told him that if the groundhog sees his shadow on this day, there will be six more weeks of winter. Not bothering to explain that, well, uh, yes . . . and if he doesn't see his shadow, there will be six more weeks of winter too, because in any event, you idiot, we have a good eight to ten weeks more of winter, no matter what that whistle pig does, shadow or not.

There must have been a certain amount of Native tipi and lodge fever because Plains Indians did their share of speculating and anticipating the arrival of spring even without a calendar hanging on the wall. The Omaha Indians marked the arrival of spring with the first thunder of the year. The Pawnee considered the kind of thunder that seems to come from all directions at once as a confirmation of spring, relying on astronomical signals first—the first sighting of two small stars they called "the swimming ducks" near the Milky Way and the positioning of the Pleiades. Having heard thunder all around during every month of the year at one time or another, I can't put any more trust in the Native traditions than those of the homesteaders. However, like most non-Natives in this new, light-polluted world, I consider myself perceptive if I

notice the disappearance of Orion in the spring sky, let alone "the swimming ducks."

The first robin sighted is often thought of as a sign of approaching spring, but, again, I find my faith betrayed. I don't know how often I have been out on a tractor moving deep drifts of heavy snow off our lane while shivering robins sat above me on the power lines, hunched up and wondering why they thought coming back north this early was a good idea. Sometimes I see them in pairs, the female of the couple apparently yelling something into the male robin's ear. I don't speak robinese, but I can pretty much tell from the tone that it's something like "I *told* you it was too early to leave Mexico and head north, but noooo, Mr. Red Breast says his no-good buddies are all leaving, so he doesn't want to be late, and besides, this year we're going to California. So when we get lost somewhere in central Texas, does he stop and ask directions from the bluebird who obviously knows where he is and where he's going? Of course not. 'We aren't lost,' says Mr. Smart Aleck, 'we just don't know where we are.'"

Slightly better indicators here seem to be the cranes and geese headed north over our place. But even then I sometimes look up when I hear them and have to chuckle because they have obviously figured out they are a bit too early and the Vs of honking and burring birds are headed back south, not north, having turned around and retreated for a least a short time to wait for more favorable and warmer winds. More reliable are the birds that come to stay, like goldfinches and house finches. They, after all, are not just passing over and headed somewhere else to enjoy spring but are relying on that season being *here*. Mourning doves are more dependable signs of spring for us, because even when we can't see them, we can hear and easily identify their cooing. *That* sound says to us that spring is darn close if it isn't quite here yet.

My own favorite avian indicator is the brown thresher with his insane song. It is one of the first we hear in the morning, always identifiable, and sure to put a grin on my face. The robin's endless, manic squawk drives me nuts, but the brown thresher is to me like the ratatat delivery of a fast-talking stand-up comedian. If you don't know the thresher's song, you have to stop and listen to it sometime. His patter is

constant and unrelenting. The thresher says everything twice, but then never repeats the couplet. To the best of my ability to take shorthand, this is approximately my own thresher's recitation as it went this morning outside our back-porch window:

Cincinnati! Cincinnati!
Bleu cheese? Bleu cheese?
Thirty weight! Thirty weight!
Pickle juice! Pickle juice!
Beer! Beer!
Pledge allegiance! Pledge allegiance!

Etcetera, on and on and on and on until sundown, every day.

While we're on the topic of biological reflections of an approaching spring, we must consider botany, which most certainly does not include the brilliant flora that explodes everywhere not long after the first of the year in the form of garden and seed catalogs. I have devoted a good part of my professional career as a folklorist to studying the history and form of the tall tale, but every year I find myself utterly outclassed in the science of mendacity as I thumb through seed catalogs. Not since the invention of the Wonder Bra has anything promised so much but delivered as little as the garden seed catalog. Not to mention the cruelty of them arriving not even remotely close to springtime but in the very bowels of winter when the contrast between the warmth, color, and beauty they guarantee and the ferocity of the Plains winter howling outside the window is at its most vivid.

Forget that nonsense about first dandelions. Dandelions are the robins of the weed world. Dandelions know zero from spring. Don't get me wrong, contrary to almost everyone else you know, I *like* dandelions. I think they are pretty. But, in fact, one of the things I admire most about dandelions is that they refuse to be bullied by things like seasons any more than they bow to the lawn worshipers' warfare against them. To me, the dandelion is not a sign of spring but a sign of tenacity in the absence of spring. Every year, just about the time I have surrendered to the inevitable and admitted that winter is indeed here—sometime around the first of December—I am walking out to the shop or machine shed and there it is, that little button of brilliant yellow, shining from the middle of the browns of winter

Even though robins are a sure sign of spring, judging from the frost on the fence post, there's still a lot of chill in the early spring air. Rick Thornton, shutterstock

dormancy or even peeking up through early snows. A dandelion, not just insistently clinging to life, but actually *blossoming*. I always pick it and take it in to Linda. For me that little flower beats the florist's finest orchid. Around February, it happens again, this time not so much a reminder of the summer that was but a promise of a spring to come, but not yet here. Not by a long shot.

The flow of sap in the maples and the time for hauling out the taps and buckets to start that first harvest of the year actually is not so much a sign of spring as its precursor. If you wait for the warmth of spring to be on the land to tap your maples, you're too late. Not to mention that the movement of sap up the inner bark of a tree is a pretty subtle indicator for all but the most intent observer. When it comes to trees, around

here I watch for the first signs of the willows along the rivers starting to show a glaring yellow, not of their leaves but of their youngest branches. That yellow is like an amber caution light at a major intersection—it not so much says that spring is here as it does that we better brace ourselves because spring and its explosion of new life is not far away.

My favorite spring flower is the lilac. I have often said that if Cindy Crawford had simply worn a lilac fragrance, she could have had me any time she wanted and not wasted her time, youth, and beauty on all those losers. The lilac is an indicator of sorts: it operates on the same photoperiod as the morel mushroom. That is, the amount and timing of light of spring that triggers the blossoming of lilacs is pretty much the same as that which coaxes the luscious

morel mushroom up from the soggy river bottom along the south side of our land. That means I don't have to go down there and wade through the downed trees to see if the morels have appeared yet. I can simply watch the lilac blooms in our backyard.

That is if there are lilac blooms in our backyard. I once got into some trouble for saying the word *damn* on national television. Three times. On a Sunday morning, I did a spring essay on my frustration with my lilacs, or more precisely with the way a late frost seems to hit my lilacs every damn year just about the time they are budding so that instead of those wonderful, pale purple blooms and devastatingly sensual perfume, I wind up with little black shrivels on the end of each twig. Again. Seems to happen every damn year.

While CBS and Charles Kuralt fielded a lot of complaints about my diction, I found I had at least two sympathetic listeners to my frustration. Kuralt himself read a couple of the letters of complaint on the air during the program and said that he thought I had used precisely the right word, because in his experience, that kind of thing *does* happen "every damn year." My favorite response, however, came from a Wyoming cowboy, who apparently also had an affection for the lilac. He wrote that far from overstating

my case, I hadn't used language strong enough! He said that the next spring, if I wanted, he would be glad to come to our place and teach me the right terms for that kind of event that he as a Wyoming cowboy knew quite well. And he promised that if I didn't get the terminology right the next time, he planned to come back whether I invited him or not, and wash my mouth out with whiskey.

I'm afraid that the problem with botanical indicators for spring is that the appearance of wild asparagus, morels, ramps, and pokeweed are not so much a sign of spring's arrival but a result of it. And what wonderful gifts they are! While we can't count on these plants telling us when spring is near, we can at least figure that when spring is near, we can start our preliminary drooling for the first edible pleasures of the season.

But enough whining about false prophets. Are there any indicators of spring's approach or arrival that we can count on? Of course there are. Just as one can calculate precisely when sweet corn is approaching its succulent prime by the fact that raccoons will harvest it first the night before you planned to pick it, you can count on running out of firewood about two to four weeks before spring arrives. Similarly, you can be sure spring's arrival is not far off when suddenly, to your amazement, you find the left mate to the right-hand insulated winter glove that went missing sometime around the first of December. Similarly, you know spring is not far off when you run across the brand-spanking new snow shovel you bought and tucked away in a place you'd be sure to find it last spring so that you'd be prepared for the winter that is now just about over. You can be sure spring is well along its way when the last tool or toy unwrapped on Christmas Day has been broken or lost.

On the other hand, you can figure you have one more good sleet or snowstorm to go after the first calves are dropped in the pasture. In fact, you could even go ahead and place bets on the fact that that last bad storm will hit the same week the calves are being dropped in the pasture! I sometimes wonder if we couldn't take steps to do some major cosmic finagling with the seasons by moving calving back a week or so every year to ensure that we get that last and worst storm over and done with earlier in the year. I do my part here on Primrose Farm by taking the chains and blade off my tractor early in March to guarantee that there are only three to four weeks of winter left and to encourage that last big winter storm to come along and be done with, which seems to work, because sure as can be, no sooner do I dismount those things and tuck them away in the trees behind the machine shed

than the snow will start to fall and the wind blow. As I once heard somewhere in another context, it happens every damn year!

Okay, if predicting and anticipating spring is a tricky business, how can we know for sure that the season is indeed upon us once it does arrive? Again, I don't pay much attention to the official indicators; like most things official, they don't have much to do with reality. But my long years, my extensive experience with rural and domestic America, and my great personal sensitivity—that's Linda you hear laughing—have taught me how to know such things. For one thing, I watch Linda. Spring cleaning is not a ritual for her; it is a pathology beyond her control. As far as I can tell, one morning she just wakes up and the demons of household cleaning are upon her. I can hear it while I am still in bed. Furniture is moved, the vacuum is running, rugs and mats heavy with winter's detritus are pitched out the door and land in the yard with a thud. If I look out the window, I can see the dogs cowering in a corner of the yard; they sense it too.

It's not just Linda; it's not just me. I was once in southeastern Germany and stopped at a small rural inn for lunch. As in this country, the best food you can get is served in small-town eateries; the smaller, the better. In Germany, you can also be fairly sure that along with making his own butter, cheese, pickles, sausage, and bread—all sublime beyond

Two horses are pulling a Deere plow through this field in Colorado in 1915. Library of Congress

Ichiro Okumura, twenty-two, from Venice, California, is thinning young plants in a two-acre field of white radishes in Manzanar, California. The photograph was taken in June 1942.
Library of Congress

belief—the innkeeper almost certainly makes his own beer. So there I was, sitting at a picnic table under an apple tree in full bloom and a-buzz with bees, facing a plate piled with a meal fit for a king—or perhaps more precisely and more desirably, fit for a farmer—and across from me sat an older gentleman, also addressing a full plate and generous stein in front of him.

After some initial consideration of our respective tasks and some preliminary samplings, we both obviously decided that the gorgeous day, scenic setting, gentle weather, and wonderful fare before us deserved plenty of time and patience. We paused between bites and struck up a conversation. My new friend introduced himself as a retiree who lived in the nearby village and, as he expressed it, a "double refugee." I asked him what a double refugee might be, and he explained that he was originally from just over the border; a Czech who fled from the Russian invasion following the aborted 1968 Prague spring revolt against Communist and Russian domination.

His story was a heroic and fascinating one with overtones of violence and disaster. When he ended his narrative, we ate a few bites more, and I finally urged him on: "But . . . a *double* refugee? Why a double refugee?"

With perfect timing and a straight face, his fork poised with a bit of sausage on the tines, he explained, "Today my wife is cleaning our house." I

understood completely and for a moment even felt a bit heroic myself.

I feel changes in my own disposition and inclinations too. For example, for me, spring means that the iron in my blood turns to lead in my butt, a condition to be cured only by dragging the hammock out of storage, putting it up, and making a list of enormous, serious problems that can be dealt with only while I am horizontal. I feel a primal urge to launder, fold, and tuck away my overalls and try to remember where I stored my shorts last autumn. And this in turn means that I need to find my sunglasses to protect my eyes from the dangerous glare of the sun. That is, the glare of the sun off my winter-white knees while I lie in the hammock in my shorts. If Linda hasn't already cornered me and prodded me into helping her with the task, it's time to do the mud porch changeover, putting away the winter coats and boots and breaking out the spring and summer workwear: lined chore coats away, lighter jackets up; heavy gloves and stocking hats to the bottom, cotton work gloves and kerchiefs to the top; snow boots to the back, light work shoes to the front.

I see it in the dogs too. They start working on their "spring complaint" by eating the first shoots of new grass out in the yard and promptly throwing them up again right in front of the front door. The most dramatic and sure sign from the dogs of the transition from winter to summer—which in most places means spring, and it does here if it lasts as long as it takes you to say the word—is their major change of venue from the sun of the backyard to the shade of the front. It's one of their rules: south side in the winter, north side in the summer. And spring is when the dogs start their annual tick collection. It's not the first tick of the clock but the first tick of spring. Of course, the first time we pick a tick off of our own bodies signals at least three months of the creepy feeling, at any time of the night or day from the slightest stray bread crumb or ladybug, that one of those infernal bloodsuckers is invading our personal space looking for a free—and these days sometimes deadly—meal. I hate 'em. Any time I hear the mindless platitude that God doesn't make junk, I bring up the subject of the tick, and the conversation goes quiet. Man, I do hate those things . . . but it is definitely spring when the first tick makes his creepy appearance.

It is clearly spring the first time the blazing new green we see out our windows as we look toward the river bottoms becomes utterly unavoidable.

It's spring when every time we leave the farm to go anywhere at all, we have to ask ourselves what we've heard about the conditions of the roads and whether it would be wiser to "take the gravel" or would it be safer to stick with the much more boring paved routes.

I know it's spring for certain the first night I open the windows, turn off the lights, crawl into bed, and hear the unmistakable but almost forgotten sounds of frogs singing down at the pond as they initiate their spring romancing.

It is spring when I wake up every morning with aches in places I had forgotten I even have.

It's spring out here in the heartland when television commercials about male enhancement potions, carrot dicers, and motorized wheelchairs are replaced with ads for seed companies, fertilizers, and irrigation systems.

It is spring when at the coffee shop in town the farmers' complaints shift from "not enough snow cover for the wheat" to "too much moisture in the ground for planting corn;" from the low price paid for last year's harvest to the high price of seed for this year's planting; from the low temperature of the air to the low temperature of the soil; and from how short the days were to how long they seem to be getting.

Spring on the Plains is, curiously, often too early for planting because the soil *is* too cold and too wet, but if we could somehow develop a measurement for the impatient fidgeting of farmers aching to get into the fields, I think we would have a reliable index of exactly how close spring is. Inevitably, at the very first opportunity, the tractors are in the fields, perhaps only testing and trying, hoping that maybe this year the seed will be in the ground a day or two earlier and the last frost holds off a little bit longer.

I sometimes wonder if some of those folks aren't out in the fields not so much for agricultural purposes but simply to get the feel of the tractor seat again and to smell the perfume of newly opened furrows. There's nothing like it unless it's the smell of that first good rain that washes away the remnants of snow, grime, and dreariness from the dying winter. Winter seems to freeze not only the sap in the trees and water in the pond but also the very smells of our tree farm. I don't know whether it is the melting snow, warmth, or southerly winds that release the smells again from their winter prisons or simply that we are once again opening our windows and letting the smells of the outdoors back into the house, but I can tell you for a fact that something happens, because a sure sign of spring is that our noses come awake as if they, too, had been asleep through the snows.

I know this is wacky, but do you know what I look for as a real sign of spring? I suspect I'm the only person in the world who considers it to be a sign of promise for the new agricultural year, but I look forward each year to the first time I am driving through the rural countryside at dusk or night, pass by a farmstead, and see the unmistakable flash and flare of a welding torch or stick. To me that means the shop doors are open and not closed against the winter's blasts. And it means the farmer under the welding mask is repairing his equipment, preparing for the campaign about to be upon him. Planting is at best a late spring or even early summer activity around here, but getting ready for the planting—*that* is the process inherent and crucial to spring on the Plains farm. To my eye, that spark and flame is like a morning star signaling the beginning of a new year in the fields, and I welcome it as enthusiastically as some people watch for the first crocus.

Robert Pripps is using a gasoline-engine drill with a 7/16-inch bit, to drill a hole in a sugar maple tree.
Grandson Noah stands by with a tap and hammer, and granddaughter Jessica is ready to hang a plastic sap bag.
Courtesy of Robert N. Pripps

MAKING MAPLE

By Robert N. Pripps

Robert N. Pripps is a tractor enthusiast who started writing books in 1989 after retiring from a career as an engineer in the aircraft industry. Robert has authored many books including The Big Book of Ford Tractors, Vintage Ford Tractors, The Big Book of Farm Tractors, *and* The Field Guide to Farmall Tractors.

After building a cabin on land he inherited from his grandfather, Robert and his family started collecting sap in the spring to make maple syrup. This hobby has turned into a successful enterprise that grows larger every year. In this essay, Robert explains the process of collecting sap and transforming it into syrup and sugar. This educational and informative piece will make you think of how the syrup you pour over your steaming buttermilk pancakes came to be. For more information go to www.prippssugarbush.com.

It's a late-February thaw and the first warm day of the year. The temperature is above freezing for the first time since early last December. It is good to be out of the house. It is even better to be in the snow-covered woods. I feel the warm sun on my back. I have snowshoes on my feet, a bright blue sky is above me, and I hear the calling of birds, from crows to chickadees. It's the time of year to head into the sugar bush.

It has been said, "If the year was less than twelve months long, no one would make maple syrup." Like other forms of agriculture, harvesting maple syrup can be arduously labor intensive, frustrating, and disappointing. But those first warm sunny days of the new year hold the promise of better times. Forgetting the pains and problems of yesteryear, it is with joy, excitement, and optimism that my family and I begin the sugaring process each year.

Just what is the process? Basically, sap is collected from the trunks of sugar maple trees (*Acer sacrum*) and boiled to remove the excess water, creating maple syrup. Further moisture removal leads to candy and then sugar. The most common way to collect the sap is by boring a 1/4- to 7/16-inch hole about two inches deep into the trunk of a maple tree and inserting a metal or plastic tap, called a spile. A bucket or plastic bag is hung on the spile to collect the sap. The tree should be at least eight inches in diameter before you begin tapping for sap. Larger producers collect sap through plastic tubing systems. The very

large producers use tubing with vacuum pumps to suck the sap from the trees. It is then pumped to a reverse-osmosis machine that removes some of the water before the sap is boiled. There are ways to remove the excess water without boiling, but strangely, the characteristic maple flavor does not develop if the sap isn't boiled.

We have a fifty-acre sugar bush in northern Wisconsin, but we're only tapping the trees on about twelve acres so far. Last year, we tapped about 1,100 trees, with mostly one tap per tree. Trees more than twelve inches in diameter can support a second tap without hurting the tree, and those more than sixteen inches in diameter can take three taps, but we have only a few trees of that size. On the best days—which entail a cold night and a warm day with bright sun—each tap will yield about two gallons of sap. Most of our sap is collected via tubing, but we have fifty buckets and bags that we put up where tubes are not convenient.

When the sun warms the tree trunks so that the snow draws back from the base of the tree we know that it is time to tap. It is important for us, being so far north, that we wait for the days to become long enough to sustain a real run of sap. Even though warm days and cold nights come as early as the last week of February, we must wait until the second week of March to get started. If we don't wait, sap will run into the tubing system, but not enough will come through to boil. Sap is only good for a couple days when the temperature is near freezing and for less

than twenty-four hours when it is warmer. Therefore, once sap is introduced to the tubing and storage tanks, it must be processed right away. If it ferments before it can be boiled, it means either cleaning the system or making off-flavor syrup. Larger producers use refrigerated storage areas and ultraviolet light to keep the sap fresh.

The water-removing process reduces the volume in a ratio of about forty gallons of sap to one gallon of syrup. The exact ratio depends on the sweetness of the sap. This can vary from year to year for reasons not fully understood. The sweetness also varies throughout the three- to six-week season. This is where some of the frustrations and disappointments come in. It may take several days of boiling before you realize the sweetness has gone from the sap, and all you are accomplishing is burning up your woodpile.

We boil the sap in a sugarhouse. Ours measures eighteen by twenty-eight feet with an L-shaped storeroom on the side. Inside is a thirty-inch by ten-foot, factory-made, wood-fired, stainless-steel evaporator with a steam hood preheater. With good sap and thirty-three inches of dry maple firewood, our rig will boil seventy gallons of sap per hour and yield almost two gallons of syrup.

It takes about 120 gallons of sap to fill the evaporator before we can start the fire. We like to have at least another 200 gallons of sap in reserve so that we can boil for about four hours. Ideally, more sap would be coming from the trees, so we can continue without interruption. Each time we allow the process to cool and reheat, the syrup becomes darker in color. Light-colored syrup is the desired result, and cooling and reheating takes a lot more firewood.

The sap level in our evaporator is controlled by float valves. The back pan, where the raw sap enters, is called the flue pan because its bottom is fluted to increase the surface area. The front pan, or syrup pan, has a flat bottom and is divided into four interconnected compartments. Partially cooked sap from the back pan enters the front pan through a float valve on the side. There it continues boiling and is pushed by the incoming liquid so that it migrates through the compartments to the opposite side of the pan. In the final compartment there is a dial thermometer and a draw-off valve. The thermometer is set to read zero when its element is immersed in pure boiling water. Thus calibrated, the thermometer goes into the syrup pan. When the thermometer's temperature is seven degrees (F) above the zero point, about a gallon of syrup can be drawn off. We also use hydrometers and optical spectrometers to check the sugar content (brix) of the syrup and sap. Before filtering and bottling syrup, the brix must be adjusted by further boiling or by

adding distilled water to the mix. Syrup that is too lean tends to mold quickly and syrup that is too rich tends to crystallize in the container.

Because we are a little too far north for ideal conditions, our seasons are usually short. Our record production is just over 200 gallons of syrup for the year. Like other forms of agriculture, if you want to make your living at it, you must be big and make a large investment in equipment! Our son, Greg, is working toward expanding our operation into a full-time business.

As with most small- and medium-sized maple producers, ours is a family affair. Many producers are full-time farmers who produce maple each spring to make use of what would otherwise be slack time. It is also a good way to take in some much-needed cash after the winter. For our family (sons, daughters-in-law, and grandchildren), however, it started because we needed an excuse to be out in the woods. We built a cabin almost thirty years ago on wooded land that I inherited from my grandfather. We enjoy it so much that we spent as much time there as possible. One year, we started dabbling with making maple syrup by using plastic milk jugs and a temporary outside boiling apparatus. (You don't want to do much boiling in the kitchen because the sap steam makes everything sticky.) The first year, we only produced a few pints of syrup. We said, "If we just spend a little money on equipment, it will be so much better."

We've said that just about every year since. Now we have five miles of tubing running through the woods, enough in sap storage tanks to hold 4,000 gallons, a sugarhouse, our second evaporator (we burned the pan on the first), a woodshed, a wood splitter, two tractors, a snowmobile, three tapping drills, three electric generators, three chainsaws, and six pairs of snowshoes. At his house in Butternut, Wisconsin, Greg has a high-pressure steam boiler, a steam finishing kettle, a pressure filter, and a steam-heated sugar-making machine. Every year, we try to expand the number of taps and improve the equipment.

Much of the sugar making process can be spread over the whole year. Filtering, bottling, labeling, sugar making, and marketing are done from the Butternut headquarters by Greg and his wife, Andrea. Every day we can spare, Greg and I cut firewood for the next season. It is best to have a year's supply on hand so that the wood is properly dried and in the woodshed for when it is needed. We have a three-bay woodshed (the center bay is for the big tractor), with each bay holding almost ten cords. For most seasons, with the amount of taps we have, ten cords will be enough to yield a maximum of 250 gallons of syrup. We are able to harvest this

This is a photograph of the Pripps' sugarhouse in the forest as steam rises in the cupola. A recent snow has left cotton ball–like puffs on branches. Courtesy of Robert N. Pripps

amount of firewood annually from our own land without decimating the sugar bush. Trees die of natural causes, wind storms blow trees over or break off the tops of trees, and, in many cases, the trees are naturally too close together and must be thinned for better syrup production.

Greg and I find the firewood production about as pleasant as any part of the maple producing process. My grandfather was a logger and sawmill owner, my father was a forest ranger, and many of my other relatives have made their livings in the timber industry. I believe harvesting wood in any form is in our genes.

The most disagreeable part of the mapling process is the cleaning. Before the boiling starts, the sugarhouse must be thoroughly cleaned from top to bottom. The state food inspector usually shows up just after we get started boiling. Besides checking for cleanliness, the inspector requires a sample of our well water. The inspector also buys a quart of our syrup from one of our retail customers for lab analysis. When the run is over, the tubing must be cleaned. We pump well water through it with induced air pressure for agitation. Starting at the tank end of the tubing run, we go to each tap, pull the tap from the tree, and let the water flow through. The tap is then placed on a plug to seal it for use next year. The bags are thrown away after use, but the aluminum buckets must be washed and stored in such a way that contaminants

The Pripps sugar bush crew. From left to right, back row: Robert, Jessica, Seth, Tyler, and Doug. From left to right, front row: Noah, Leah, and Hannah. Courtesy of Robert N. Pripps

cannot enter. Likewise, the storage tanks must be cleaned and sealed until the next year.

Making maple syrup and sugar is a process that dates back hundreds of years. According to the journals of early explorers, Native Americans made maple syrup and maple sugar. They called it *sinzibuckwud* (drawn from the wood). Sap from maple trees was gathered by chopping the trunk of a maple tree with a tomahawk to form a V-shaped slit and catching the

Greg feeds wood into the evaporator. The amount of steam rising from the front pan indicates a good boil. The back pan has a steam hood and pipe so that its steam goes directly out of the cupola on top of the sugarhouse. The evaporator fire consumes about three wheelbarrows of wood each hour. Courtesy of Robert N. Pripps

sap in small birch-bark baskets. There is some anthropological disagreement as to how the Native Americans actually converted the sap into sugar. One school of thought is that early European explorers introduced metal containers for boiling. There seems to be no evidence that the Native Americans made use of the maple sap prior to the fifteenth century, which lends credence to this postulation. The other school of thought says that they poured the sap into hollowed out logs or stone troughs and brought the sap to a boil by dropping in hot rocks from a nearby fire. And we think we have it hard today! Because Native Americans had no easy way to store liquid

syrup, they made most of it into maple sugar, which was easily stored for later use.

When the New England colonists arrived, the Native Americans showed them how to make maple sugar, and it became their principal sweetener. Sometimes as much as a thousand pounds of sugar was made per family. The valuable excess provided income because it could be sold or traded for other food and supplies.

Up until the later part of the twentieth century, the retail price of a gallon of syrup was the same as the average daily wage for a working man. Today it runs to less than half the average daily wage, because

About two gallons of sap have dripped into this bucket during an eight-hour period. The sap is as clear as water and has a slightly sweet taste. Courtesy of Robert N. Pripps

> *In the spring, at the end of the day,*
> *you should smell like dirt.*
> **—Margaret Atwood**

process improvements have reduced the amount of labor involved. As late as the 1920s, more maple sugar was sold than maple syrup. Beet and cane sugar eventually took over as the most popular sweeteners and maple sugar became very hard to find. As the price of cane sugar began to undercut maple sugar prices, many sugar makers made the shift to producing more maple syrup, a luxury item, and less maple sugar. Because maple sugar is now a rare commodity, that is Greg's direction for the future of his business. Plus, shipping of sugar to the far reaches of the world is much easier than shipping syrup. Pripps maple products have found their way to Russia and Europe.

Like all forms of farming, mapling is dependent upon the weather. During one season, the daily temperature reached seventy degrees with eighteen inches of snow still on the ground. Needless to say, that was a very short sap run. When the maple trees start to bud, production stops because the sap's flavor changes. There is a general rule that says the more severe the winter, the better the sap season. Another rule is that a dry summer or a winter without much snow makes for a poor season. The only rule that I know that holds in every case is that none of the other rules do! With so many factors beyond human control, it is hard to be an atheist farmer of any kind.

Making maple syrup and sugar may not sound like a lot of fun to some people. As most producers will be quick to report, there are rewards other than financial that keep us coming back year after year. The greatest incentive is maple-syrup-drenched buttermilk pancakes. Sure, we could buy the syrup, but it would not be the same. Another incentive, which was what drew our clan to it, is the joy of the woods and the appreciation of God's beautiful creation. Syrup season is also a great way to spend time with my family. Because it often coincides with Easter break from school, the grandchildren are able to come to help in the process. Finally, it is the love of chopping firewood that makes it all worthwhile. I believe it is our frustrated logger-genes that pull us into the forest to feel the bite of the chainsaw into wood and the shout of "TIMBER" as another tree comes down.

Greg and his son Tyler are tapping trees with a 5/16-inch drill bit for the tubing runs. In this operation, the sap runs by gravity to holding tanks.
Courtesy of Robert N. Pripps

Men from the Horse Shoe Forestry Co. are pouring maple sap into gathering tanks. This photo was taken in St. Lawrence County, New York, circa 1901.
Library of Congress

This outbuilding basks in the morning sun in the Arkansas Ozark Mountains. Lee Klancher

My Father's Flock

By Michael Perry

Michael Perry is a humorist and author of the best-selling memoir Population 485: Meeting Your Neighbors One Siren at a Time, *the essay collection* Off Main Street, *and the memoir* Truck: A Love Story. *Michael has written for* Esquire, The New York Times Magazine, Outside, Backpacker, Orion, *and* Salon.com, *and is a contributing editor to* Men's Health. *His essays have been heard on NPR's* All Things Considered, *and he has performed and produced two live audience recordings (*I Got It from the Cows *and* Never Stand Behind a Sneezing Cow*). Michael lives in rural Wisconsin, where he remains active as a volunteer firefighter and emergency medical responder. He can be found online at www.sneezingcow.com.*

Raised on a small dairy farm, Michael equates his writing career to cleaning calf pens—just keep shoveling and eventually you've got a pile so big, someone will notice. In this essay, Michael helps during lambing season at his parents' farm while his dad is recliner-bound due to a knee injury. His childhood memories, mixed with the present, and sharing the joy of lambing season with his daughter provide an insight into the miracles shepherds encounter every spring.

Long before my farmer father had cows or cornfields, he was a shepherd. Last March marked his fortieth lambing season. The sense of anniversary was monkey-wrenched during the first week when, as he climbed aboard a tractor (something he has done almost daily during those decades), the knee of his trailing leg emitted a celeriac crunch, which, as it turned out, was the sound of his meniscus dismantling. He was instantly hobbled with pain, unable to bear weight on that leg, and confined to the recliner. We kids—all grown up now—took turns staying at the farm to help out.

Lambing season amounts to a month of insufficient catnaps. You tromp to the sheep shed every couple of hours, around the clock, for four weeks straight until the last ewe delivers. Each time you enter the shed you're looking for a sheep giving signs of imminent birth. She may be pawing the straw, walking in circles, or simply looking distracted. An ewe experiencing the early twinges of labor will sequester herself along a wall or in a corner. At the commencement of a contraction, the otherwise placid animal will extend her neck, raise her head, roll back her upper lip, and wrinkle her nose. A laboring ewe will grunt softly, as if she is being nudged in the belly (I hear a chorus of female voices: *As she is, Einstein!*). Another means of early detection is to put out fresh hay. As her compatriots rush the feeders like woolly pigs, watch for the ewe who remains apart—she's next.

Midwifery-wise, your basic job is to stay out of the way. Observe from a quiet remove and let nature take its course. Recede. Wait.

From my largely oblivious childhood perspective, Dad's sheep were a sideline, whereas cows required our daily attention. When you weren't working with the cows, you were working on chores predicated on cows. Sheep, on the other hand, spent most of the year as distant gray lumps in the outermost pastures, forgotten until the occasional faint bleat floated in from the back forty. In the warmer months, they required little more than watering. If they were close by, we dragged out the green garden hose. If they were in outlying pastures, we transported the water in old milk cans. In the deeper parts of winter, we would take them hay daily, busting bales over the snow. A few times a year there would be worming sessions during which we also gave vaccinations and trimmed hooves. The summer worming sessions always took on a rodeo feel, as we would quite literally shepherd the sheep from one pasture to another,

This late spring photograph of a newly sprouted cornfield is a wonderful sight to a farmer. It's a sign of things to come in what one hopes will be a bountiful crop. Gordana Sermek, shutterstock

Opposite:
Kentucky native Vince Siler is a ranch mechanic and carpenter who lives near Great Falls, Montana. Lee Klancher

sometimes detouring unexpectedly down the county road; all those frantic hooves on the asphalt set up a scuffy little clatter.

In the early part of the year, however, the sheep begin to wedge their way back into the schedule until they dominate. In February, Dad sets up the pens and feeders and gathers the flock to be shorn, after which—having lost their winter coats—they take up permanent residence in the lambing shed until spring when the grass returns.

Dad frequently refers to himself as a "dumb sheep farmer," but he loves his "woolies," as he calls them. Once when someone suggested that sheep were not so bright, he said, "Y'know how you make a cow? Inflate a sheep, paint it black and white, add two faucets, and remove its brain." He was gentle with all of his animals, but I suspect the sheep speak

to him on a level the cows never did. This may be tied to his faith and the presence of sheep in the Bible, something which I have never inquired about but should put on the list of Before It's Too Late. What I do know is the cows are gone, and the sheep remain, and someone must watch over them. Tonight it's me.

When the alarm sounds at 2:00 a.m. (rousing by habit and intuition, Dad rarely requires the uncouth tool), every lazy bone in my body—to say nothing of my cotton-bound brain—assumes a specific gravity designed to drive me deeper abed. I summon the strength to rise only by conjuring the fantasy of how sweet it will feel to drift off upon my return. By the time I am dressed and downstairs, I am reanimating my childhood. On weekend nights, we kids were allowed to rise and accompany Mom or Dad on midnight

Leslie Tripp speaks with two guests on her 13,000-acre ranch near Great Falls, Montana. "It's a great place to raise kids," she said. "I don't think they'd be as well-adjusted living anywhere else." Lee Klancher

maternity rounds. There was always a feeling of anticipation coming down to the dark kitchen and bundling up for the trek to the barn. Beyond the weak pool of the yardlight, the farm was socked in darkness. Wisconsin's March is highly variable. Sometimes a soft wind was soughing in the pines, shushing through the needles and pushing the scent of melt. Sometimes the night was clear and deep-frozen. Sometimes snow was coming down. One night when big flakes were lazing past the yardlight like feathers from a burst pillow, I went to check the sheep with Mom. While she held the iron gate open, I stepped through and the top of my head brushed the underside of her outstretched arm. "My goodness," she said. "Pretty soon you won't fit under there!" I felt eight feet tall and strode the rest of the path with shoulders squared. When I married two

When the April wind wakes the call for the soil, I hold the plough as my only hold upon the earth, and, as I follow through the fresh and fragrant furrow, I am planted with every footstep, growing, budding, blooming into a spirit of spring.
–Dallas Lore Sharp

years ago, I was given a daughter named Amy who is now just six years old but growing fast. The top of her head has already reached my sternum, and the day when she won't fit beneath my arm is fast approaching. This is her first lambing season, and I was happy yesterday when she walked with me to the barn, and we found a sheep ready to deliver. I told her she could name the lamb.

The lambs are named alphabetically. The practice dates back to my childhood and was always a fun game. I remember long-gone fuzzballs named Herkimer and Knucklehead and Lillelukelani. Adherence to the alphabetical constraints was

Sheep graze contentedly in their pasture as their shepherdess looks on. Daniel Johnson

jovially strict and resulted in fuzzy little creatures named X-ray and Zapata. The ledger of record was a clipboard hung on a nail. The pencil dangled on a string. The system remains unchanged.

In the barn, Amy was eager and attentive, watching closely and asking questions as the lamb emerged. It was stillborn. She cried a little, and we talked about it. Two hours later, she returned, this time to see twin lambs arrive alive. As they shook themselves and tottered to life, Amy smiled and chattered brightly. While I have attempted a career out of overthinking things, I suspect her smile was all the wider in light of her recently acquired prior knowledge.

I love the sheep barn at night. The animals are settled, resting like woolly boulders with their legs folded and hooves tucked beneath their bodies. If you stand in the quiet, you will hear them chewing their cuds. The sound of human mastication drives me nuts in a split second, but for some reason, the sound of sheep chewing in the nocturnal quiet calms

me. An animal in distress does not work its cud, and all that muffled molar work—with regular pauses to swallow one bolus and raise another—sends a subliminal message of contentment. When I was young, I would climb the haystack into the rafters, curl up, and simply listen.

Tonight I hear an infantile bleat before I reach the barn, and when I straddle the fence and cross to the straw, I find a young ewe lying on her side and straining. There is a fresh-born lamb beside her, and as I approach, she presses out another. It arrives in a slithery amniotic gush and plops wetly to the straw. Encircling its nose with my fingers, I milk its nostrils and mouth clear of fluid, then stand back to watch its ribs bow in and out as the first hacking breaths transpire. By the time it shakes its ears loose (this always reminds me of an accelerated version of the emergent butterfly uncrinkling its wet wings after escaping the chrysalis), I am experiencing the standard moment of marvel at how the whole deal

This curious sheep pokes its face through a fence to keep track of the spring activities around the farm.
Paulette Johnson

works. The ewe has turned, snuffling and chuckling as she licks the amniotic fluid away, roughing and fluffing the tight wool curls so they can air-dry. As usual, the other sheep ignore the goings-on, with the occasional exception of the yearling ewes. Having never given birth, they sometimes sniff the lambs or the hind end of the laboring ewe curiously, their ears cocked forward in a mixture of curiosity and alarm.

Dad keeps a baby food jar filled with iodine in the barn, and I retrieve it now, removing the cap and lifting each lamb so I can thread the umbilicus into the iodine. I do it how I remember seeing Dad do it, clapping the jar tightly against the lamb's belly, then tipping it back so the umbilicus gets a good soak. The lamb is left with a circular orange stain on its abdomen. The practice prevents navel ill. In a week or so, the umbilicus will turn to jerky and eventually drop unnoticed to the straw.

By the time I have finished, the ewe has gone to pushing again. I ease around behind her. I'm hoping to see a soft pair of hoof tips cradling a little lamb snoot. The hooves are there, sure enough, but they are dewclaws-up and there is no snoot. Bad sign. These are the back legs. Breech delivery. I hustle back to the house and wake Mom. Dad has always shouldered the bulk of the lambing chores, but defers to my mother for tricky deliveries. A registered nurse, she comes armed with delivery room experience and delicate hands. Dad's hands are not over-large, but they have a sausage-y thickness brought on by manual labor and are therefore poorly suited for navigating obstetrical tangles.

I get back to the barn before Mom and find the ewe panting and the lamb half out—its head, shoulders, and front legs are still lodged in the birth canal. It appears there is no time to wait, so I grab the lamb and pull it the rest of the way out. Its head is still

An ewe and lamb are a sure sign of spring on a farm.
Paulette Johnson

inside the amniotic sac. I clear the nostrils and mouth, but there is no breath. I give a couple of pushes on the ribs and dangle the lamb by its back legs, which looks drastic, but it allows fluid to drain from the air passages. When I place the lamb on the straw, its flanks flutter, and then I hear the familiar crackle of air working into the lungs. Shoot, the little feller's off and running. Mom arrives. Minutes later the lamb gives a high-pitched bleat, and I am just plumb happy.

We stand and observe, let the new family get to know one another. Mom kneels behind the sheep and checks inside to rule out quadruplets. Nothing. The ewe's long push is over. Using another trick my father taught me, I guide the sheep to the pen by dangling the third lamb in my hands while slowly backing across the barn and into the small square pen. It takes a while. The mother wants to dart back and forth between lambs, so I carry two and Mom the other. Soon they are ensconced, the two oldest lambs already stumbling about in their jabby-stabby knock-kneed way. The breech lamb is worn out. After watching the first two lambs suckle, we try to help him latch on, but he's tuckered. Dad says the emerging thinking is that immediate nursing isn't as necessary as previously thought, so we'll leave and let the family settle. Over the course of the coming day, we'll keep an eye on the little guy and make sure he learns how to get his dinner. Mom jots the ewe's ear tag number and the sex of each lamb on the clipboard, but we leave the name spaces blank. Amy can name them in the morning.

Forest Kellison, a 4-H club member, raised this sheep to exhibit at the fair. He is seen here examining the quality of the fleece under the direction of Harold Willey, a Farm Bureau agent. This photo was taken by Lewis W. Hine in Pocahontas County, West Virginia, on October 7, 1921. Library of Congress

Opposite:
Lambing is a very busy time for anyone who raises sheep, but seeing adorable lambs, such as this, frolic in the lush, green pasture, is all worth it. Norvia Behling

We return to the house. The frozen air is bell-jar still. The sky is deep black; the stars press down brilliantly all around. At the age of forty-one, walking beside my mother, I feel young and old at once. I am reminded that we are not beneath the stars, but among them.

When I was a young boy and accompanied Dad to do the checks, once the lambs were dipped and penned and the clipboard filled, and we were back in the house, he would disappear into the cellar and come back up with a Mason jar of canned dewberries. We'd share a bowl of the sweet berries, the dark red juice in the bowl reminding me of the iodine in the baby food jar.

These sheep are being driven into town (Winchester, Kentucky) on August 5, 1916. Library of Congress

Tonight there are no dewberries. Mom is off to bed, and I cross to the kitchen sink where I begin to scrub my hands. I am soaping up when I realize my wedding ring is missing. It must have come off during the delivery when my hands were slick with amniotic fluid. I grab a flashlight, retrace my steps, and spend a good hour diligently searching the straw. Nothing. A week later, I return with a metal detector and try again. Still nothing. Spring arrives. Dad's knee heals, the sheep return to the far pastures (accompanied now by galumphing, growing lambs), and it comes time to clean the barn. I drive to the farm and make one more pass with the metal detector. A rusty nail, a rusty hinge, and nothing more. Dad moves in with the skid steer and begins loading out the manure.

Married for over a year, and already I've lost my wedding ring. Some wise guy asks me if I checked inside the ewe. Well, no. But perhaps this year we can expect a little miracle lamb—born with a golden band around one ear. I've notified my father and put him on watch. His knee is holding up, and this year it will be him out there around the clock. Forty-two years a father, forty-one years a shepherd, and always, his eye on the flock.

Chapter 2

Summer

In June, as many as a dozen species may burst their buds on a single day. No man can heed all of these anniversaries; no man can ignore all of them.
–Aldo Leopold

Summer on the farm means endless hours in the field and haymow. The steamy, humid weather can be relentless, but sitting in the shade with an ice-cold beverage in hand can provide instant relief. After a long day full of hard work, there's nothing like sitting on the porch in the darkness, watching the fireflies dance across the yard, and listening to the frogs sing their nightly chorus in the nearby creek.

Homegrown watermelons are a refreshing treat during the hot summer days. Kenneth and Linda Glaser, pictured with the ever-present farm dog, relax in the shade on a late summer day in 1951. Courtesy of Kenneth and Shirley Glaser

Farms buzz with activity during the summer. There are always many tasks to accomplish during the lush growing season. Daniel Johnson

Auction attendees carefully peruse this lineup of implements. Paulette Johnson

Learning How to Walk Through Life One Auction at a Time

By Jessie Kay Bylander

Jessie Kay Bylander was born and raised in River Falls, Wisconsin, and spent many days of her youth playing in a grain bin or leaping off the tops of round bales—even though she and her brothers were expressly told not to do either of those things.

While mother-daughter bonding often comes naturally, daddy-daughter days can prove more and more difficult as adolescence sets in. A love of commerce and hot dogs cooked by church ladies provided a common ground for Jessie and her dad. But no bonding with a parent can be done without learning some hard lessons as well.

I first learned about the cruelties of life—at least those pertaining to capitalism—at a farm auction I attended with my father. I was five years old or so. I'm sure the goal of attending the auction, which I recall as being a sprawling, rolling estate that smelled like horse manure and sunshine, was to pick up semi-rusted gardening implements or perhaps a chainsaw. But like any five-year-old girl, I fell victim to the curse that weighs on all five-year-old girls: I saw a horse and was struck down by love. I *wanted* that horse.

My dad, victim to the curse that weighs on all fathers, wanted to give his little girl a horse. But he is a pragmatic man, and though I'm sure his heart was breaking as he asked, he probably knew my answer would not be remotely realistic.

"What should I bid on the horse?" he asked.

My reply: "Forty dollars."

My dad's recollection is that the bidding started at three hundred. Legend has it, I cried all the way through the rest of the auction. A year later, I fell off a horse at my friend's farm, and I developed a lifelong fear of horses. This sort of impulsiveness that results in fate taking a hand will sadly become a theme.

Auction season, like garage sale season, runs from early April to early October, with the peak months being June to August. Back during my attendance years, I knew it was time to gear up for hours in the sun when I saw the *Shopper* folded into a long, vertical quarter, perfectly framing a black-and-white-and-

yellow-all-over auction bill notated in my dad's impenetrable code of double underlines, circles, and bold rectangles—an era ended when my dad discovered pastel highlighters.

Under the sometimes insufferable Wisconsin sun, my dad and I wandered through acres of flatbed wagons stacked with mildewing crates of untold treasures and machine shed lineups of hoes, shovels, and rakes. It was amongst these items that I learned one of the most important rules of auction-going: do not demonstrate any interest in the object you desire. My father attended one auction purely for the chance to gaze upon an antique corn sheller. When we finally stood in front of the crooked, odd-looking gadget, I said, "*That's* what you're here for?" My dad looked across at the gnarled old farmer who was also circling the sheller. The wrinkled face looked back at him impassably. My dad said, and I believe this is not paraphrased, "Hmm."

As we strolled away, Dad explained to me that even if you feel your soul will wilt and die without the item, you never do anything more than circle it twice and eye it, maybe examine a portion of it if you're feeling particularly saucy (these are my words, not his). You do not squeal with delight and clap your hands. You do not talk to anyone else looking at the item, though I believe this is not applicable to tractors, as no man seems able to resist talking shop about tractors.

The rat-a-tat rapport of auctioneers might sound like gibberish to some, but to savvy auction attendees, it's a symphony that ends with the glorious word SOLD! Paulette Johnson

I also learned that these rules applied to the actual bidding process. Auction handlers and callers, like bristly, feed-hat-wearing sharks swimming in a junk-filled sea, can smell desire and profit like the slightest hint of blood. Midwestern farmers are notoriously stingy, but if even the tiniest possibility presents that testosterone will be allowed to take over years and years of penny-pinching, even-tempered behavior, the handlers will sink their walking stick-cum-pointers into that cracked door and swing it wide open. The trick, my dad said, is to nod tightly and firmly and keep your hands down. If the price comes within spitting distance of the absolute maximum you have settled on in your head, you curtly shake your head a few times, but keep eye contact with the handler who is, more than likely exclusively, handling your bid. If you feel the item is truly worth pursuing, bend a bit. If it passes your maximum, break eye contact and turn away.

My father was theorem in motion. Curt? I probably watched my father exchange ten to twenty words with the auctioneer crews in ten years. Firm? A snort and turn from my father immediately sent the bid out into the ether. In fact, I believed that if my father performed that move, there *was* no real winner of the item.

One area where I did not need lessons and which I anticipated every summer, whether run by church club, 4-H group, or homemakers' circle, was the auction cuisine. I inherited Dad's deep love and appreciation of the summer menu: sloppy joes (on sesame seed bun, if you were at a more upscale auction) and slow-cooker hot dogs, fat and sweaty and covered in ketchup and raw onions. A bed of baked beans or potato chips on Styrofoam place settings were potential sides, but sometimes the sandwiches were simply handed over on a pillow of napkins. These delicacies were eaten in the full glare of the sun if Dad was

An auction sign on the side of the road is a common sight along country roads in the summer. Many stop by for curiosity, or they may know the owner, and sometimes the allure of auction cuisine is reason enough to pull in and check things out. Paulette Johnson

accepting of summer's embrace, or in the shade if Dad was tired of the expletive-expletive flies and the sweat trickling down his neck, and washed down with a dripping can of Dr. Pepper that inevitably gave both Dad and me violent hiccups. Another trait I inherited from Dad, along with the appreciation of 4-H–prepared cuisine, is the ability to inhale it at Hoover-exploding rates with deep swallows of carbonated beverages, and then hiccup until spurred into an expletive-laden outburst. Regardless of how boring the advanced course in It Looks Like It'll Fall Apart When Putting It in the Bed of the Truck, But…, I would hang in there for the inevitable trip back to the food booth before they closed up shop.

Following my father through those summers was like a cost-free seminar in how to walk through life, not just auctions. When I reached sixteen, I had been taught to buy and live with my cards close to my chest

and act frugally and calmly. Get what you want, but want things that are practical and useful.

You know the Merle Haggard song about how his protagonist turned twenty-one in prison doing life without parole and no one could steer him right? You can't say that daddy didn't try.

When I turned seventeen, instead of committing a felony punishable by twenty-five to life, I signed up for my own bidding number at a large estate auction. I fancied myself something of a budding collector of farm antiques. Dad had purchased several rusty milk cans for me the summer before, and with elbow grease and spray paint, I had renovated and turned them into blue-collar-chic yard items. With my own number in hand, I had my heart set on a copper boiler.

I saw it under a maple tree. It was glorious, all wooden handles and tarnished body. I very well could have gaped at it for fifteen minutes. My checkbook,

This field is currently full of empty pickup trucks, but most of these trucks will cart home a great find. Paulette Johnson

Summer has set in with its usual severity.
–Samuel Taylor Coleridge

Oh, the power a bidding number holds. The heady mix of anticipation and permanent marker is a powerful thing for a first-time bidder. Paulette Johnson

full of funds earned at the local hotel laundry, was burning a hole in my purse, which I clutched at my side.

My father was somewhere across the way looking at plows and potato planters. The auction, as it often happens at large estate sales, had split into two roving bands: one following the farm equipment and the other following the "household" items—in other words, the junk that is of interest to ladies and antique collectors. It was simply me, armed with my potently Sharpied number on a stiff placard and a dream of refinishing that copper boiler and selling it back to an antique dealer for a staggering profit.

The bidding started at fifty. Remembering my father's instructions to wait until the price bottomed out, I did not wildly wave my number. However, when the auctioneer hollered ten dollars, I entered the bidding. Probably, if I am honest, it was with a full-body spasm.

The sound of corn leaves blowing in the wind is part of the soundtrack of summer. JoLin, shutterstock

The blood, it was in the water.

A lady across from me threw her hat in the ring. My nerves were on fire. The price bounced in five-dollar increments until it stood at forty. The increments dropped to two-fifty, but the lady, my mortal enemy for nearly five minutes, backed out and wouldn't budge. The copper boiler was mine.

I went to the trailer, signed my check with flair, and walked back to collect my copper boiler. But somewhere between first glance and the pistols-at-dawn currency duel to possess it, it had undergone a spooky transformation, like some reverse Dorian Gray. The copper boiler was pockmarked with about one hundred BB indents. It had been used for target practice. The handles were rank with rot. It was a lemon. A lemon that looked like an acne-ravaged elderly man interpreted as a washtub.

My dad, returning from across the lawn empty-handed, looked at my purchase and asked how much I had paid. To try and reenact my father's ice-cream-headache expression would not do it justice.

Ten-plus summers later, I used my cell phone to call my father from the Lake County, Indiana, 4-H auction to report that the auctioneer had *both* kinds of handlers: the "YUP!" guy *and* the "HO!" guy. Not to be confused with the current urban vernacular "ho," the auctioneer helper "ho!" is more along the lines of the Shakespearean, "What ho! Is this a gallon of goat's milk I see before me?" My dad laughed at my yelping imitations, and the air was heavy with the scent of sloppy joes. There was a towheaded boy wandering the stands with a cardboard box full of ice-cold sodas and, as a representative of the changing times, bottled waters. Between my father and me were miles divided by my new hometown of Chicago, where auctions are mostly silent, something I have never been able to wrap my head around. I mean, how does your adrenaline get moving without YUPs and HOs? True, the auctions are held for charity, something I applaud, though I imagine the prices would give me an expression similar to my father's copper-boiler-for-WHAT? face. I am still miserable at controlling my impulses

Farmers listen to an auctioneer list the wonderful qualities of a cow up for sale at this auction outside of Appleton, Wisconsin, in 1954. Wisconsin Historical Society

when it comes to items I want; I buy DVDs, CDs, and books in bulk from Amazon.com at least once a month, not to mention the impromptu trips to the local thrift stores, half-price bookstores, and Targets.

The collected efforts of my antique collecting career reside in the basement of Dad's house. I believe the copper boiler actually lives out in the barn somewhere, no doubt destined to be purchased in a future auction for far more than it is worth. Although I still love the occasional boiled hot dog—I do live in Chicago, after all—I've learned to cook with tofu now and then. But through it all, what I remember, mostly through his words, is that we were once the team that walked through a long-ago summer and attempted to buy a riding horse for forty dollars. A horse that I wouldn't have wanted a year later, just like that damn copper boiler.

Growing up on a farm, your playmates consist of siblings and neighbor kids. This foursome spent many summer days together. Brothers George (standing) and Kenneth (far right) and brothers Everett (left) and Ron (middle) were neighbors as well as distant cousins, circa early 1940s. Courtesy of Kenneth and Shirley Glaser

Chores seem to multiply during the summer. This farm girl is filling up water buckets for her horses. Daniel Johnson

One of the bonuses of life on a farm is growing your own garden. Carrots, peas, beans, tomatoes, and the like come to life and will provide the farm family with food throughout the long, cold winter. Paulette Johnson

There are always a few glorious summer days when all of the chores are done (or could wait a day), and one can indulge in some leisure time. For Bill Glaser, any free time in the summer was spent fishing. He caught this German brown trout near Boyceville, Wisconsin, in the early 1950s. *Courtesy of Kenneth and Shirley Glaser*

How sweet I roamed from field to field and tasted all the summer's pride.
–William Blake

Bill and Kenneth Glaser show off their bounty from a day full of fishing, circa mid-1950s. Courtesy of Kenneth and Shirley Glaser

The Country Drifters are performing at the Barneveld, Wisconsin, Legion Hall on October 20, 1973. The band was composed of Dale Storkson (guitar and vocals), Leo Loy (accordion), and Joe Loy (drums). This group of farmers and a trucker played at various dances and occasions in the community. Courtesy of Henry and Ruth Berg

FRANK, PINKY, AND HARRY

By Jerry Apps

A professor emeritus of agriculture at the University of Wisconsin–Madison, Jerry Apps has written more than thirty-five books, many of them on rural history and country life. Recent titles include the best-selling Country Wisdom, Every Farm Tells a Story: A Tale of Family Farm Values, *and* Living a Country Year: Wit and Wisdom from the Good Old Days. *His writing has earned awards from the State Historical Society of Wisconsin, the Wisconsin Library Association, and Barnes and Noble booksellers, among others. Jerry and his wife, Ruth, have three grown children. They split their time between their home in Madison, Wisconsin, and their farm near Wild Rose, Wisconsin.*

In this essay, Jerry tells us the story of Frank, Pinky, and Harry: three musicians who performed at many local gatherings and entranced a young Jerry one hot summer night.

You could hear the sound of music a half-mile away, especially on a hot summer day when there was no wind, and dust lifted from the country road and hung in the air like a dirty blanket. The music ranged from polkas and waltzes and schottisches to more haunting tunes that reminded the musician and his wife of the Old Country of Czechoslovakia.

Almost every Sunday afternoon in the summer, Frank Kolka took out his concertina (some of the neighbors called it a squeezebox), sat on a chair, and played beautiful music. He played for his family—Mrs. Kolka had been born in Czechoslovakia—and for any neighbors who might be driving by. And he played for himself, as he leaned back in his chair, worked the fifty-one buttons on the instrument, and let the music flow. Each button played a different note on the push and the pull.

While my brothers and I attended Chain O' Lake School, we got to know the Kolka boys, Jim and Dave, very well. They lived only a mile from our farm, straight to the west as the crow flies and a little farther by road because the road has a few twists and turns and went up and down a couple of hills along the way. Jim was half a year younger than I was; his brother was a couple years younger. They were the closest kids to our farm, and Sundays were a good time to visit them.

I remember the first time my brothers and I heard the music when we were walking along the road to their farm on a Sunday afternoon. It sounded like a radio playing in the distance, and I said that to my brothers, who also could hear the sound.

"But it can't be a radio," I said. "Plays only music, and it's so clear—no static." Nobody could listen to a radio in our neighborhood without picking up static; the radio stations were just too far away. The exception was at night, especially a winter night. Then some of the stations came in strong and clear, especially WGN and WLS out of Chicago.

When we reached the top of the hill, from which we could see the Kolkas' farmhouse in the distance, the music became even clearer. As we walked along, we could see Frank on the porch, squeezing away on something from which beautiful music came. His long fingers bounced around the keyboard. A smile spread across his tanned, weathered face. After greeting Jim and Dave, I pointed to the instrument and asked what it was called.

"It's a Pearl Queen concertina," Frank answered. "Any particular tune you wanna hear?"

I said I didn't know any songs for him to play. I didn't know much about music. The only songs I was familiar with were "Red River Valley" and "She'll Be Coming 'Round the Mountain," tunes I had heard on the WLS Barn Dance from Chicago on Saturday night. But I didn't want to mention those songs, because he seemed to be playing a different kind of music.

Frank began playing again, pushing and pulling on this rather unusual instrument with buttons on

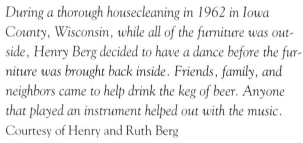

During a thorough housecleaning in 1962 in Iowa County, Wisconsin, while all of the furniture was outside, Henry Berg decided to have a dance before the furniture was brought back inside. Friends, family, and neighbors came to help drink the keg of beer. Anyone that played an instrument helped out with the music. Courtesy of Henry and Ruth Berg

Cousins Jean and Ray Berg played at an event in Waunakee, Wisconsin, in 1966. They played everything from Ethnic Swiss Yodel Waltz/Norwegian Dance Tunes to Country Western. Courtesy of Henry and Ruth Berg

each side and a leatherlike material in the middle that folded and unfolded when he pushed and pulled on it. Soon all of us were tapping our feet to the music, allowing it to become a part of us. This was the first time I had heard polka music and old-time waltzes, as some people called them. Outside of the WLS program, the only music I had listened to was church organ music, and that was about as exciting as walking in deep mud. Of course, there was piano music at school, which was sometimes fun but often not.

Frank's music was fun. It was exciting. It had a beat. It was something you wanted to listen to. And it had a lot of variation; going from fast to slow, from quiet to raucous, from happy to sad. Frank played "Red Wing," "The Red Handkerchief Waltz," and "Springtime in the Rockies." He played "The Barbara Polka" (his wife's name was Barbara) and "The Pond

Lily Waltz." And he mixed in Czech tunes. Tunes from the Old Country. Tunes that evoked memories.

When we returned home that afternoon, I told Pa about Frank and his concertina.

"Yup. Frank can make that squeezebox talk," Pa said. "Sometime I gotta take you someplace where Harry is playing his fiddle."

Pa then told me about Harry Banks, whom I knew because he lived right across the road from Kolkas' farm. I knew that Harry, an Englishman, tall and thin, was a farmer and part of the threshing crew that came to our farm, but I hadn't heard about his fiddle playing.

"Few people play the fiddle like Harry," Pa said.

"How does he do it?" I asked.

"Harry caught his hand in a hay mower a few years ago. It cut off a finger on his left hand."

It was not an unusual accident. Many of the farmers I knew had parts of fingers missing, a lot of scars from

Alfred Wittwer, shown with his dog, Mickey, is playing a three-row button Swiss accordion. Most Swiss accordions were handmade in Switzerland and cost around $80 in the 1930s. Alfred entertained family and friends in the late 1940s to mid-1950s with songs from his homeland of Switzerland and sang in his native language and yodeled.
Courtesy of Henry and Ruth Berg

being cut, and sometimes entire hands and even arms missing because of farm accidents.

"You gotta give it to Harry," Pa said. "He doesn't let a missing finger on his left hand stop his fiddle playing. He taught himself to play with three fingers."

While I was pondering how someone could play fiddle with only three fingers, Pa brought up another neighbor who played an instrument.

"Bet you don't know that Pinky Eserhut plays the banjo," Pa said.

I didn't know much about Pinky Eserhut. I didn't even know how he got his first name, which seemed a bit strange, even in our rural community where there were many unusual names. Pa explained that Pinky's hair was a kind of reddish color, which was probably the reason for his name. His real first name was Alvin.

I didn't know anything about banjos and what kind of music they made. Pa didn't play an instrument and didn't know much about music, but he tried to explain that a banjo was something like a guitar and had strings, a bigger end, and a longer neck that was attached to it.

The age when children started playing the accordion was not the main factor as much as the child's size and ability to handle the instrument. If a family had a three-quarter size accordion or a "student-size" (with smaller keys to fit the child), the child could start playing at a younger age.
Courtesy of Henry and Ruth Berg

He said that the bigger end was like a little drum with a piece of leather stretched across it. When you strummed the strings, the sound was like a cross between a guitar and a drum.

Pa went on to tell me that from time to time Frank, Pinky, and Harry came together as a band and played for wedding dances, birthday parties, or any other occasion for which a group of people gathered to have some fun.

As good fortune would have it, Bill and Lorraine Miller were celebrating their wedding anniversary the following Saturday night, and we were all invited— Ma, Pa, my twin brothers, and me. This would give me a chance to see the local band perform, and it was my first chance to see people dancing to polka and old-time waltz music.

By the time we arrived at the Chain O' Lake School, somebody had already moved all the desks to the side, and the three musicians were up in front,

Country dances were a popular social activity for rural folks during the summer. This dance took place in McIntosh County, Oklahoma, circa 1939.
Library of Congress

tuning their instruments. At least that's what Ma said when I asked her what they were doing.

Cars were pulling up in the schoolyard, the women were gathering inside, and the men were standing around the front steps, smoking their pipes and sharing stories about their corn and cows and the price of potatoes.

My twin brothers, who were nearly four years younger than I was, trailed behind Ma inside the schoolhouse. I stayed outside with Pa. But we weren't out there long before the band began playing the first number. I asked Pa what it was, and he said he

thought it was "The Beer Barrel Polka." But since he didn't dance much he said I should ask Bill Miller. Bill was too busy celebrating his anniversary to answer such a question, so I didn't ask. I just found myself a seat next to the water cooler and watched with considerable amazement.

The people here were folks I knew, our neighbors in the Chain O' Lake community, but I had never seen them dance. Couples were swinging around the floor, hopping ever so often like jackrabbits and stamping their feet like I thought the floor might break. Polka dancing looked like hard work, especially on a warm summer evening. Nobody seemed bothered by the temperature, though; they were all grinning from ear to ear as they hopped around the floor in time with the music. Even Mrs. York was out there dancing with her husband, Guy, and she was smiling. I didn't remember that I'd ever seen her smile, but she was this evening. Something about polka music, I decided, seemed to lift the worries off people's backs. I knew there was plenty to worry about. It hadn't rained much all summer, the hay was short, the corn plants could scarcely keep ahead of the weeds, and the oat crop, especially on the hilly farms, was mighty slim. No matter. Everybody was dancing the polka.

I focused my attention on the band, trying to figure out how such wonderful music could come from three farmers. Frank Kolka sat in the middle of the threesome, his concertina on his lap. Harry Banks,

the three-fingered fiddler, stood to his right, and Pinky Eserhut, all decked out in a red shirt and a new pair of bib overalls, sat on the other side of Frank. There wasn't a scrap of printed music anywhere. All three of them played by ear, picking up tunes as they heard them. They were having fun making music, such beautiful music as I had never heard before.

They played three polkas in a row and then stopped to check with each other about what to play next. Looking around the room, I thought that some of the dancers were gonna keel over either from becoming overheated or from overexertion. I hadn't seen so much sweat since the last time we threshed.

The dancers had scarcely moved from the center of the floor when the band slipped into an old-time waltz. Now, an old-time waltz isn't all that much slower than a polka, but there is less hopping and no foot pounding. I suspect some city visitor might say the waltz is a more civilized kind of dance than the polka. But there is surely nothing uncivilized about the polka once you know something about it and appreciate the fine music that's necessary for dancing it.

As the evening moved on, the music became sweeter and finer, at least that's how it sounded to me.

> *Rest is not idleness, and to lie sometimes on the grass under trees on a summer's day, listening to the murmur of the water, or watching the clouds float across the sky, is by no means a waste of time.*
> **–John Lubbock**

You could almost feel people's problems lift from their shoulders. You could see the transformation, too, in people's faces, in their laughter, and in the lightness of their steps.

Before the evening was over, I found myself liking the music from this little three-piece band even better than the WLS Barn Dance from Chicago. Maybe it was because I could see the three musicians as well as hear them. Maybe it was because there weren't any breaks to advertise cow feed or Keystone barbed wire. Maybe because Frank, Pinky, and Harry taught me that music is good for more things than tapping your toes. On this one night, people put their problems aside and experienced the joy of living, a feeling that was mighty scarce in our community during bad years.

The chickens on the Bill and Mildred Glaser farm are used to the boys on the farm. George, Wallace, and Kenneth are pictured among the farm's poultry in the summer of 1941. Courtesy of Kenneth and Shirley Glaser

Family gatherings and reunions frequently happened on summer Sunday afternoons. It was common to have the relatives over for dinner and a leisurely afternoon after church services. Sisters-in-law Christine and Hannah Eliason sit on the lawn of the Bill and Mildred Glaser farm, circa late 1940s, and are undoubtedly listening to someone tell a story. Courtesy of Kenneth and Shirley Glaser

Eight-year-old Jack is milking a cow on his parents' farm in western Massachusetts. Lewis W. Hine took this photograph in August 1940. Library of Congress

Ah, summer, what power you have to make us suffer and like it.
–Russell Baker

A curious Jersey noses up to the camera on a sunny summer day. Jerseys are smaller than Holsteins and are known for high quality milk. John, shutterstock

Calves are a very popular animal to raise and exhibit in 4-H and FFA competitions. They can be stubborn little animals, but if you start training calves when they are young, by the time they are older, they are seasoned pros in the show ring. Norvia Behling

Chickens are a very versatile animal on the farm. They can be used to fertilize and cultivate small portions of land, produce eggs, and provide meat for the freezer. Paulette Johnson

Goats have become a very popular sight on farms. Those who don't have the time or space for cattle can opt for maintaining a goat herd. Daniel Johnson

Picking fruit and vegetables from your own garden is a very satisfying experience. Knowing that you nurtured and cultivated the food with your own two hands is a powerful feeling. Daniel Johnson

A Tough and Hardy Breed
By Bob Becker

Farming isn't just for men. For hundreds of years, women have toiled in fields and barns alongside their husbands, fathers, or brothers. On top of keeping the house clean, raising the children, and putting food on the table three times a day, women help all around the farm. Bob Becker tells us about his grandmother and aunts as they toiled their way through the summer. Gardening, raising chickens, and canning were some of the duties Bob remembers the women had during his childhood.

Late July, early August . . . this time of year always seems to bring back a few memories of the farm women in my life, back when I was a youngster. Right about now, as the crops ripen on our farms, recollections of the parts my mother, grandmothers, and aunts played each summer in the harvesting activities come sifting back. Long hours and a mountain of hard work, that's what women knew.

Take gardening, for instance. The farms, I recall back then, were almost totally self-sufficient. Not much food was bought at the store. Thus, big gardens were the rule; lots of peas and beans, carrots, beets, plenty of

Farm women are a tough and hardy breed. This farm woman from Evergreen, North Carolina, was photographed in April 1915. These women always found time to keep the house clean, feed everyone, and help out in the barn and fields.
Library of Congress

tomatoes, and usually strawberry and raspberry patches, too.

By August, the bounty from the earth would be building. Yet in those 1930 times, the home freezer, upon which most of us depend so heavily today, didn't exist. In fact, in my country home back then, electricity didn't even exist.

The ladies would start to talk about "canning time" and an annual frenzy of preserving fruits and vegetables for the winter ahead would begin. Down from the attic would come the pressure cooker, a machine that had an aura of danger attached to it, complete with warnings of how it could explode as it huffed and puffed on a wood-burning kitchen range.

Up from the basement would come boxes of blue Mason jars, the kind with a name embossed on the side. Today they've become collector items at flea markets. The jars and their gray metal lids would be boiled to sterilize, and a fresh supply of sealing rings made of red rubber was laid out.

From the garden would come the bushel baskets of tomatoes and the milk pails of peas. For days on end, it seemed, the ladies would toil in their kitchens, steaming and hot in ninety-degree summer temperatures.

At the end of the day, long rows of shiny and glistening jars of freshly canned vegetables would rest on clean dish towels on the kitchen table, waiting for their lids to pop, the signal

Do your part

that they'd cooled sufficiently and sealed properly and could be taken to the wooden shelves in the basement for storage.

Mixed in with canning would be the normal, daily duties of cooking and serving three meals for the menfolk(who were busy putting up a second crop of alfalfa) and keeping an eye on the young kids.

Raising poultry was often another of the ladies' jobs. Each summer, my grandmother grew a sizeable number of chickens, ducks, geese, and occasionally a turkey or two. The job started in the spring with her setting hens; they went from clutches of fluffy chicks and ducklings trailing behind the old clucking hens to plump, full-feathered birds as the summer wore on.

Each evening before dark, she'd make her rounds to inspect her flock. First to the hen house to gather the eggs from her leghorns in a peach basket she carried on her arm; she sold the eggs for a little private income of her own.

Then she went on to the fenced pens to assure that her other young charges had been properly fed and watered by my uncles.

Grandma's weekends? Well, Saturdays, they didn't count. They were just another workday. Sundays? Well, Sunday afternoons were when a passel of big city relatives always dropped in for a visit . . . and to stay for supper, of course.

If it wasn't relatives stopping by, it would be a church picnic, which was an event where every lady in the parish was expected to pitch in. There'd be cakes and pies to be baked in advance. On the big day, long hours were spent peeling, boiling, and mashing potatoes; frying a seemingly endless supply of chicken; and serving the hundreds that came to eat. And all of these duties were done in stifling hot kitchens on hot summer days.

I think back today with great admiration to those long-ago farm women. They were a tough and hardy breed.

Baling hay has become considerably easier and faster with automatic balers that kick the hay bales into the wagon. A group can be unloading hay at the farm while someone is baling another load in the field. Cathleen Clapper, shutterstock

The Church of Cold Beer, Wrestling, and Women of Questionable Virtue

By Lee Klancher

Born and raised on the banks of the Brill River in northern Wisconsin, Lee Klancher spent thirteen years working as an editor at MBI Publishing Company while writing and taking photos in his free time. He left the corporate world in late 2006 to pursue his freelance career full-time.

One of the time-honored summer traditions on the farm is haying. Lee grew up near Brill, Wisconsin, as a teacher's kid surrounded by farmers. In this piece, he reminisces about his days wrestling, drinking beer, and haying with a cast of characters who whipped him (sometimes literally) into a proper Wisconsin boy.

I've spent a good part of the past ten years driving down some of this country's least-traveled roads, as most of my assignments lead me to lightly populated corners of the world where there's more traffic from tractors than automobiles. I like seeing these forgotten nooks and crannies and take a distinct pleasure in finding what's interesting about places that most people don't even know exist. When I'm bouncing along down a beat-up strip of gravel, and the forest gives way to fields, one of the pleasures of the journey comes a few hours after a farmer has cut his hay field.

The smell of freshly cut hay is one of the unique olfactory experiences that takes most country kids—even one with the dubious fortune of being raised by teachers and surrounded by farmers—right back to haying days.

Haying was a part of my summers growing up near Brill, Wisconsin, a part of the season as inevitable as going back to school or base-running drills during Tuesday night softball practices. Putting up hay was a high-grade form of farm work torture, the kind of thing that a few twisted souls might get misty-eyed about, but if they were sent back there to do it again, they'd curse the time travel gods and wish for a hammock and a six-pack or maybe a day at the dentist—anything besides throwing around fifty-pound bales in a blast furnace of a July day.

For me, haying is more than just another manual-labor-intensive reason for farmers of the 1970s to procreate rather than hire. The truth is, when I think of haying, I think of cold beer, wrestling, and women of questionable virtue.

I can explain.

I grew up a few miles north of Brill, a town of roughly fifty souls in the center of northwestern Wisconsin. Our place was on the banks above the Brill River, a little trout stream spanned by an old metal bridge that rattled like a paint mixer shaking a can full of bolts when a car load of high school kids crossed it at forty-five miles an hour, speeding towards a beer party in the gravel pit or some other nefarious destination.

The area was a mix of open farm fields and the wooded river valley, with the fields giving way to hardwood forest a few miles to the north. Neighbors were few and far between, with less than a half-dozen dairy farms scattered around our country-mile-long "block."

We lived a long way from anything even vaguely urban, literally as well as metaphorically. My parents taught in the "big" town of Rice Lake (pop. 7,698), which was thirteen miles from our little house. The nearest real city was Minneapolis, which was a two-and-a-half-hour drive away. We went there once every two or three years, usually to catch a Twins–Brewers game.

I grew up as a teacher's kid who could read at age four and was surrounded by farm kids who drove

Whenever the farm truck starts up, the farm dogs are right there and anxious for a trip to town. This Australian shepherd enjoys riding shotgun, along with an open window, on the jaunt to town. Norvia Behling

tractors at age five. In the neighborhood, at least, this made me a bit of a pariah.

From late June to early September, a lot of the farm kids' summer days were spent making hay. It's hot, dirty work, and I took a lot of guff from them about the fact teacher's kids didn't have to do that.

Once in a while, just to keep my neighbors off my back, I'd pitch in and help my friends hay. Part of that was because I was a kid and I wanted to hang out with other kids, and part of that was to take on the impossible task of shaking the teacher's son stigma.

Before sixth grade, I was not just a teacher's kid. I was a chubby, small, unathletic teacher's kid. This was nearly social suicide for a kid from Brill. If you couldn't unload the hay wagon as fast as your old man, you at least needed to be able to hit a softball further than one of the Hovde kids.

I struck out on both of those fronts. I was the best speller in the class, but that didn't mean much in Brill, Wisconsin, in 1975, especially to those who

lived on farms. The farm-kid ethic was the ability to work long days and attend to your responsibilities. A boy who spent afternoons reading, trout fishing, or tearing around the neighborhood on a dirt bike was nothing more than lazy—that was made clear to me at an early age.

In the summer between sixth and seventh grade, my body stretched from five-foot-one pudgy to five-foot-eight muscular. I would grow only another two inches in my journey from seventh grade to adulthood, but for a few glorious years, I was a giant. I won arm wrestling contests. I was taller than most of my friends. It was great.

My perception of who I was stretched along with my body. I felt that, for the first time in my life, I was equipped to compete in those games of strength and skill that establish pecking order on the playground at the Brill grade school.

During the summer, pecking order was established on the haywagon. The haywagon in my neighborhood

Farm dogs deserve a rest after a long day of work. Wherever the farmer goes, so does the dog. This Welsh corgi, a breed used for herding cattle, takes a break at the end of a long day of haying. Daniel Johnson

was about half a mile from my house at the Cherney place down the road. The Cherneys were our nearest neighbors with kids. There were four boys in the family, and the youngest one, Bobby, was in the same grade as me. Bobby and I both liked motorcycles, and we hung out during the summer.

We started riding motorcycles when we were eleven years old. We both had similar Honda motorcycles that were almost always breaking down. We spent as much time riding as we did trying to weld, wire, or duct tape the bikes so that they'd run, but that was part of the fun.

When we were thirteen years old, we conned our parents into buying us used motorcycles, early 1970s

Honda 100cc bikes that had clutches, five-speed transmissions, and lights. The first day on those bikes, we met at his house at 5:00 a.m. with plans to ride all glorious day. At that early hour, the grass was still slick with dew, and we both crashed when the tires slid on the grass in the pasture across the road from Bobby's house. I was trapped under the bike with my leg pinned against the muffler. By the time I pried the bike off my leg, the hot muffler burned through my jeans and into my leg. The burn left an oval scar on my right calf that you can still see. The burn hurt like hell, but I was so happy to be on a "real" motorcycle that I didn't care.

Some of the time during the summer, I had free time and Bobby had chores, so I'd help him out. I'd hang out with him and feed the calves and haul manure. That was one of Bobby's jobs—to haul manure (only in Cherney-speak it was never "manure," it was

71

Many hours of the summer season are spent in the seat of a tractor. It is a beautiful place to soak in a sunset.
Daniel Johnson

"shit." And the "manure spreader" was the "shit spreader"—always). He drove the tractor under the conveyor on the back side of the barn, filled it up with manure (shit), and off we went to the field to spread it out.

That was Bobby's job, incidentally, because he was good at driving tractors. Being the youngest, he had driven tractors since he was five or six years old. He could back an eight-foot-wide four-wheel trailer through a nine-foot-wide shed door in one smooth shot and leave it parked perfectly square to the wall, every time. He could speed-shift a tractor and lift the front wheels off the ground. He could do tractor wheelies.

In fact, Bobby won the tractor-driving contest held at our school. Word on the street was he would have gone on to the national tractor-driving competition, but his scores on the written part of the test weren't good enough to qualify.

The tractor was a tool that Bobby was perfectly suited to operate, a piece of machinery that fit him as naturally as a thumb-softened paintbrush to Rembrandt's hand or a Leica range finder to Henri Cartier-Bresson's eye.

"Helping" Bobby haul manure or feed calves mostly entailed standing around and talking, and maybe grabbing a pail or a pitchfork here or there. Haying was another matter. It was the Big Kahuna of farm chores, harder work than cutting wood or mending fences. The only work that really compared, that could inspire the same level of awe and dread, was picking rock. To do that, a tractor and wagon would creep along across a field and the unhappy victims (usually kids) walked behind the wagon and picked the larger stones out of the field and threw them on the wagon.

I picked rock once in my life at another neighbor's farm. I was invited over to play with the

The connection between a person and a horse is a very spiritual one. They work side by side on the farm in a definite mutual-respect relationship. Daniel Johnson

Ekstrom kids, and next thing I knew, I was out in the field slinging stones onto the back of a wagon. When you live in farm country, beware of invites to come over and "play." That word doesn't mean what you think it should.

Haying had the same aura as rock picking—it was hard, hot work—but it wasn't as mind numbing as picking rock. Heavy equipment was involved—balers, rakes, tractors, elevators, and wagons. Running machinery appeals to me. I still enjoy working with our tractors at our cabin, and just being around all that machinery lent an air of adventure to haying.

Haying is also vigorous, hard work, with moments of heavy labor and downtime for sitting in the shade and telling jokes. Like working out or writing, a day of putting up hay left you with a sense of accomplishment.

So when I knew a day of haying was coming, I often found excuses to go home and fish or read or do

some of the other things teacher's kids do when farm kids are working. But some days, I hung around and helped out.

In fact, I hung around with Bobby enough to develop a farm kid's appreciation for rain. Rain meant no haying, which meant time to screw off rather than work.

To this day, a rainy midsummer day represents a break to me, a time to do whatever utterly useless activity I want to do in the house: play video games, watch movies starring Burt Reynolds or Clint Eastwood and a monkey, listen to my Electric Light Orchestra albums. Those brain-dead Sundays are precious, and I suspect my appreciation for a stolen day originated on summer afternoons when rain bought us a reprieve from haying so we could spend the day inside playing cards or watching the Muppets.

When the day was clear and the hay was dry, we spent the day haying. I don't remember spending a

Dogs aren't the only hard workers on the farm. Cats are constantly on the prowl to rid the farm and barn of any rodents. Barn cats are also wonderful pets. This farm girl takes time to bask in the sun with a favorite barn cat. Norvia Behling

lot of time helping out with haying until after my growth spurt. I looked at it as a time to test out my new capabilities and find out if I was made of sterner stuff than being the last kid in the footrace around the playground at Brill School.

Jobs when haying have a definite hierarchy. The bottom of the barrel was driving the tractor. That was hot work, as the sun beat down on you mercilessly as you sat on a tractor seat for anywhere from six to twelve hours, but it didn't require a lot of physical exertion. If the radio on the tractor happened to be working, you could crank it up and blast music loud enough to just make out the words and a few guitar riffs over the engine's drone. I'd assume most farmers with radios on tractors without cabs are deaf by now. Seriously.

*The summer morn is bright and fresh,
the birds are darting by as if they loved to breast
the breeze that sweeps the cool clear sky.*
–William C. Bryant

When working for another friend's uncle one summer, I raked hay with a little Ford tractor (without a radio). I enjoyed driving the tractor, but was no tractor genius. The farmer scolded me for running the tractor's engine too high in the rev range and for raking too fast. I didn't have the gift.

When haying on the Cherney farm, Bobby drove the tractor when he was younger and too small to toss around hay bales. Once he was big enough to handle a bale of hay, others drove the tractor, and he was moved to more physical labor.

When hay is baled, it's done with a baler, a piece of machinery that is towed behind a tractor. The hay is lifted off of the field by the baler, and the machine compacts the hay into squares. The squares are bound into bales that are two feet high, two feet wide, and four feet long. The baler ties the bales together with two pieces of binder twine.

A bale of hay weighs between forty and fifty pounds dry and eighty and one hundred pounds if baled when the hay is damp. This meant that handling the bales—either stacking the wagon or unloading the wagon—was a job for larger, stronger kids. And handling wet hay bales can and will tear out your back.

The cast of characters at the Cherney farm included all four Cherney brothers: Dan, Jim, Gary, and Bobby. Gary was the oldest. He had an arm that was crippled, and he often worked up in the mow or drove the tractor. The most responsible at that time, Gary pretty much ran the farm. We all knew he'd be the one to take it over (and he did). Gary had a live-in girlfriend who stayed at the farm, and he managed to spend a few of his Saturday nights at home. He was the kinder, gentler member of the family. He gave us goofy nicknames and did his best to keep Jim and Dan from killing Bobby.

Dan and Jim were the middle brothers, and they did a lot of the heavy lifting (when not trying to kill Bobby). Both of them were rough characters, guys who drove jacked-up four-wheel-drive trucks and showed up for Sunday morning chores hung-over and battered.

They were in their late teens in my haying days, and both were built like kegs of beer, with square, broad shoulders, beefy arms and forearms, and the beginnings of beer bellies. Jim was a bit cleaner cut with sandy blond hair cut short and a dark tan. Jim was also the meaner of the two. He liked to spend his weekends drinking hard and fighting harder.

One morning, when I had stayed overnight at Bobby's house, we came out to the milk house to get ready to do the morning milking, and Jim was out there already. I think he came home just in time to milk. He had three broken fingers and fresh cuts on his knuckles. His hands looked like they had been caught in a meat grinder. He had this rakish grin, and I can remember him flashing that as he told us, "You should see the other guy—he went to the hospital."

Jim played varsity sports in high school, had good-looking girlfriends, and had some minor skirmishes with the law. He wasn't around all that much, because he was either off with his girlfriend, on a bender, or (on occasion) locked up for the night.

Dan was a few years younger and had dark hair, bad skin, and a foul countenance. He used to look for excuses to whale on Bobby, particularly. I'd occasionally catch a stray punch as well due to some perceived slight.

Entrances were one of Dan's strengths. I'd be over at Bobby's after school, more often than not trying to repair one of our old motorcycles in the little white shed on the Cherney farm. Dan would drive home from school, usually in his giant, green Chevrolet 4x4 pickup. Dan's vehicles were lightly muffled, to say the least, and he announced his return to the farm by thundering down the hill to the Cherney farm, the truck's engine spitting and backfiring as he rolled up to the turnoff from the blacktop to the gravel road that ran past the farm.

The sound of that unmuffled V-8 engine signified the end of the few minutes of peaceful existence Bobby and I had. Dan would roar into the yard, slide out of the truck door—his truck was jacked up so high he fell out of the truck as much as stepped—and sloop-shouldered his way toward the house. On good days, he would give us a sidelong glance and toss a profanity-laden insult or two our way on the way in.

On not-so-good days, he'd come and gift us with a steady stream of verbal torment, generally directed at our lack of intelligence, manhood, or mechanical ability. On bad days, he'd dispense with the niceties and just start whaling on Bobby or me or both. Dan's random acts of violence gave him a dangerous aura. He could make you cringe just by walking in the room.

Dan and Jim were both at their best when it was haying time. Like a couple of sled dogs who would tear each other to bits in camp but are focused and intense when pulling hard in the traces, the edge came off the two of them when they made hay.

That isn't to say they didn't still have a well of aggression. One of the duties of making hay is stacking the hay in the wagons as it is baled (which didn't always happen—sometimes the hay was just tossed into the wagon to land in a jumbled pile). If we were on stacking duty, we inevitably found ourselves with a little

The saying "Make hay while the sun shines" is very true. With an occupation that is dependent on the weather, sometimes the window to bale hay is a very short one. Days when hay can be baled are most often very long, but it's worth it to get hay that hasn't been rained on into the haymow. Daniel Johnson

Opposite:
Rainbows are a beautiful way to mark the end of a much-needed rainfall during the summer. Farmers might need a bit of cheer if cut hay was lying on the field during the rainfall. Brandon Sanders, shutterstock

downtime while the full wagons were hauled back to the farm. Downtime for Dan and Jim usually meant trouble.

One warm summer day, we were cutting the hay off a field near PeeWee's Tavern, a bar with a softball field, about five miles from my home. The group was Bobby, me, Dan, and Jim.

We had a break of about an hour because we had all the wagons loaded and were ahead of the group unloading at the barn. The tractor was gone, and it was the four of us, sitting in the shade of one of the full hay wagons waiting to be hauled in and unloaded.

The boys got bored and decided it was time for some physical activity. Jim wrestled in high school, as did I. And Dan just plain liked to mix it up, so an impromptu

wrestling match started, with the winner staying in and losers going out. Dan whaled on Bobby for a while, with his objective not to win but to inflict pain and (hopefully) extract tears. Then Jim tagged in.

Jim was a pretty good wrestler, a quick and strong 180-pounder who knew the moves. He took Dan out in fairly short order; his superior knowledge of the sport quickly overcame Dan's uncontrolled brute force.

Then I was up, thirty pounds lighter but younger and motivated by fourteen years of weenie-hood. I don't remember being able to beat Jim, but I held my own against him and managed a takedown or two. For the once-pudgy, taking down a nineteen-year-old brute made for a pretty fine day.

Unloading and stacking hay bales are two perennial summer tasks that many bemoan, but it's a very satisfying feeling to look at a full haymow and know that your animals will have food throughout the long winter. Daniel Johnson

That day loading wagons was an exception, however. The job you'd most likely find Dan (or Jim) doing was unloading the wagon. This was the big dog of haying jobs, work that made your shoulders ache for days. The bales of hay would be pulled off the wagon and placed onto a hay elevator, which carried the bales up into the barn's haymow.

Clearing off the hay wagon was hard work, as the bales were usually not stacked, just tossed into the wagon by the baler. You'd grab the forty- to fifty-pound bales by the twine that bound the compacted slabs of hay together and heave them up and toss them on the elevator.

Wisconsin summers can be hot and sticky, and that annual bout of hot, humid weather always seemed to come around during haying season.

Temperatures could hit ninety-plus-degrees with ninety-plus-points of humidity.

Heaving heavy bales in the saunalike weather, you quickly became covered in sweat. The sweat captured the loose hay and covered you in a coat of small brittle bits of chaff. The chaff would break or irritate your skin and create a nasty rash. Shorts kept you cool, but the chaff that crawled into your nether regions was so uncomfortable that some chose to wear long pants.

By the end of a day spent putting up hay, you looked like a shaved Sasquatch with a three-day growth of green stubble growing over a near-terminal case of guttate psoriasis.

At the top of the elevator, three or four guys would stack the hay into the mow. Someone experienced had to be directing the operation up top. The hay had to be stacked so that it would ventilate and dry. If stacked improperly, the hay would spoil. If you really screwed up the job, the curing stacks of hay could heat up to the point where a fire started.

The haymow was hot and foul and full of hay chaff. On a ninety-degree day, it might be one hundred-plus in the haymow. Some barns were equipped with a fan or two, but mows are big places, and even a giant barn fan has a limited effect on the temperature.

The speed of the process was determined by how fast the guy on the bottom could unload the wagon. Generally, if you had enough people in the mow, they could handle what the guy below could put on the elevator. The faster the guy on the bottom did the job, the sooner the whole crew was done. A quick unload meant a few more minutes to sit in the shade of the barn and relax until the next load came in, so there was a premium on having speed in the wagon.

I was about fourteen when I was first asked to unload the wagon. I can remember one of the boys, I think it was Gary, sizing me up and saying, "Klunker's grown up a bit. I think it's time he unloaded that wagon for us." So into the wagon I went, and I put my heart and soul into throwing those bales off as quickly as I could. The boys would time themselves to see who could unload the wagon the fastest. As I recall, Jim was the fastest. My times were nowhere near Dan and Jim's, but they were quick enough that I kept the job for a day here and there.

At the end of a long day unloading hay with the Cherney boys, a group of us was sitting and relaxing in the Cherney house entryway, and Bobby's mom, Marilyn, brought out cold bottles of Old Milwaukee for us.

"If you boys are old enough to work that hard, you are old enough to have a beer," she said as she passed the bead-sweated bottles.

I had sipped beer here and there before in my life, stealing a bit from my dad's glass or sneaking a can in the basement with my friends. It always tasted bitter, and I can remember thinking I would never actually like drinking beer.

The ice-cold lager tasted just right that day, and I felt, for the first time in my nerdy little life, like a kid who could pass for a man. I was sitting in the entryway of the Cherney's old farmhouse, leaning a hard-backed chair back against the old faux-wood paneling. That entryway reminds me a lot of my grandfather's little den in the basement, a place

Diane Stehr drives her father's John Deere during the 1951 haying season. The Stehr Farm was located near Balsam Lake, Wisconsin. Diane was about ten years old at the time. Lee Klancher Collection

Three Saunders children, ages nine, eleven, and thirteen, are pitching grain out of the mow. Lewis W. Hines took this photograph in August 1915. Library of Congress

where Grandma let him hang his mounted deer heads, antlers, and beer signs. I guess I'll always associate cheap wood paneling with manhood.

One other night stands out in my haying memories. I'd like to think it was the same day that Ma Cherney brought us those icy Old Mils, but I'm not sure that's correct. It was a summer night, and we had been haying that day. A big group of my friends, kids from all over the extended Brill neighborhood, and I were there. As I recall, there were eight or ten of us playing out in the yard.

Bobby was there, of course, plus me and Bobby's cousins, Brad and Sharon Drost. The Drost kids were a bit shadier than the Cherneys, the kind of kids who made you believe that their scrapes with the law might not just be kids having too much fun but a lifelong occupation.

Brad was a smart-talking, bandy little guy whose mouth never stopped, with dark olive skin, a stick-thin build, and omnipresent cowboy boots. He was a year younger than me. His sister, Sharon, was two years older. Sharon shared his olive skin and dark hair, but her build was noticeably more curvaceous

than Brad's, and she had a notoriously rough wit. In fact, she was notorious for a lot of things, most of them prurient and probably the rural myths inspired by imaginative fourteen-year-old boys. Whatever the truth of the matter, we all knew she ran with a fast crowd. In our minds, she was a woman of ill repute.

On a warm summer night, the kind where you never want to go in because the air is so sweet and cool, we were in the yard playing hide-and-seek. That's a great game on the farm, as a big yard with lots of outbuildings becomes a giant, mysterious playground in the dark.

Late that night, I found the perfect hiding place in a partially full hay wagon covered by a tarp. Under the tarp was a comfortable space to hide. In that space, I found Sharon. She had a full beer stolen from the Cherney fridge, and she invited me to come in.

We hid there for a while. An hour? Two? Twenty minutes? I don't know. I do know that everyone had assumptions about what happened when they did finally find us. Those assumptions were wrong, incidentally—nothing happened beyond a conversation.

Carl Brown was eleven years old when this photo was taken by Lewis W. Hine in August 1915. Carl and his father ran a farm of 160 acres in southern Vermont. Library of Congress

Eight-year-old Jack drives a load of hay on his father's farm in western Massachusetts. Lewis W. Hine photographed Jack in August 1915. Library of Congress

Whatever the perception, the reality was I had spent a dark, cool evening in a confined space with a woman of ill repute—sharing a beer, no less.

I walked a bit taller the next day.

Does that juvenile moment explain why the smell of hay makes me happy? I don't think so. I believe part of the reason I love those lost back roads is they are home to me. Driving a country road today reassures me that the things that mattered when I was a kid still matter in certain parts of the world.

The sweetly acidic smell of fresh-cut hay always makes me smile and roll down the window to breathe it in. I don't think of Bobby, or of Sharon, or even of that first cold beer. Mostly, it's a pleasant odor that takes me back to a time when your place

in the world could be established with a wrestling match in a hay field.

Haying to me is about more than putting away something to feed the cattle. It's about finding a place in a world where I didn't quite fit. It's about growing from boy to young man, crossing those borders that define that boundary, or at least those that did to a kid from Brill, Wisconsin. It's about discovering a rough-and-tumble side of me that I still value.

For a kid whose grade school days were spent chasing the pack, the ability to measure up in an environment where your strengths are largely regarded as a waste of time was more than satisfying. It was a passage, my confirmation in the church of rural Wisconsin.

CHAPTER 3

Autumn

For man, autumn is a time of harvest, of gathering together.
For nature, it is a time of sowing, of scattering abroad.
–Edwin Way Teale

Autumn's fiery-colored trees help warm the soul from the chill in the air. The smiles that radiate from bright orange jack-o-lanterns evoke nostalgic memories of trick-or-treating. The dry cornstalks that rattle in the autumn winds are a soundtrack for the harvest season. The smell of wood smoke permeates the air as woodstoves are fired up to chase away the crisp coolness of the season. Scarecrows dot the countryside with their welcoming faces. Every warm Indian summer day is spent outside in order to extract one more ounce of warmth before the cold winter winds settle in.

The family is in awe at the lovely Thanksgiving dinner Mother is placing on the table in this illustration from the 1952 International Harvester calendar.

Opposite:
The bright, beautiful fall colors provide a sharp contrast against this Wisconsin pasture. Daniel Johnson

Scarecrows have evolved from a useful garden tool to an autumnal icon. Daniel Johnson

SCARECROWS ON THE FARM: IMAGES OF A RURAL AUTUMN

By Samantha Johnson

Samantha Johnson is the author of The Field Guide to Rabbits, *and the co-author of* How to Raise Horses. *Her articles have appeared in several horse- and farm-related publications. Samantha is a horse show judge, certified with the Wisconsin State Horse Council and the Welsh Pony & Cob Society of America, and she raises Welsh Mountain Ponies in northern Wisconsin. She enjoys gardening (especially heirloom vegetables), bird watching, equine color genetics, and foaling season when she is kept busy while attending the birthing mares.*

Living on a farm since childhood has allowed Samantha to form an appreciation for all of the seasons and their impact on farm life. She has a special affection for the autumn harvest season, as captured in the following essay. Scarecrows, as Samantha describes, represent everything that is cherished about the change of seasons. Whether working in the fields or decorating the porch, scarecrows are beloved by many and are truly the epitome of autumn.

When autumn arrives in the rural United States—on the farms, ranches, and small villages of this great country—beautiful things happen. Meadows turn gold, crops mature, corn ripens, and the stalks make a crisp, rustling sound. The intensely blue sky forms a backdrop for the trees while they perform their last hurrah of the year with an impressive display of oranges, reds, and yellows. Children gleefully jump into piles of freshly raked leaves, laughing as the leaves burst into the air like colorful fireworks. Goldenrod and asters dot the roadsides, bringing a sudden glow of purple and gold at a time when all of the other flowers have returned to their season of slumber. Families partake in the age-old tradition of jack-o-lantern carving, reaping the reward of watching as the candlelight flickers through the crevices of the pumpkin. Long afternoons spent in the Indian summer sun stretch lazily into evenings that have a hint of frost.

Other beauties that characterize autumn on the farm include overflowing bushel baskets of apples, trees filled with apples of different shapes and flavors, winter and summer squash in enough varieties to satisfy everyone, small yellow squash with crooked ends, long green squash with white speckles, round yellow squash with scalloped edges, and creamy-colored squash the precise shade of butter. Children run, giggle, and chase each another through corn mazes. Long afternoons are spent outdoors, while the shadows sharpen and the golden sun casts its haze on smiling faces.

The steady march of days wears on, the harvest is in, corn is stacked high in the cribs, tomatoes are canned, and apples and potatoes hibernate in the cellar. A winter's supply of hay is stacked in the barn; farmers breathe a silent prayer of thanks as the barn doors swing shut. After the whirlwind pace of summertime and the long days spent weeding gardens, putting up hay, and harvesting crops, the precise, rhythmic flow of days resumes. The days are no longer sporadically punctuated by quick meals on the porch, devoured rapidly in an attempt to get back to work. The days begin growing shorter, as does the list of daily chores. Children head back to school. The place they so hurriedly abandoned at the beginning of summer now seems like a haven of rest and continuity. In short, the hustling, hard-working season of summer is followed by its gracious successor: autumn.

It is also in autumn that scarecrows come into their own. Of course, the farm families have been using them throughout the spring and summer months. These oddly dressed creatures are stationed in appropriate locations near gardens and fields, but it is only now that the rest of the world begins to

Smiling scarecrows dot the rural landscape throughout the fall season. They are often propped next to a shock of corn-stalks. Daniel Johnson

notice and admire them. Suddenly, against that sweeping backdrop of maturing autumn, we see the scarecrows standing out in all their haphazard glory. Scarecrows are a truly rural innovation. Perhaps they are not as historically important as some of the other advancements produced by rural minds, such as the cotton gin or the milking machine, but they are nonetheless steeped in tradition and laden with charm and are important to the farm in their own way. As with so many other fixtures of farm life, we can easily take these complacent creatures for granted. Like a sturdy fence post or a reliable tractor, scarecrows are always there and always will be. Their presence is never questioned, their worth never truly appreciated. Yet when we pause for a moment to reflect on the scarecrow's status and importance on the farm, we begin to realize that the scarecrow, weather-beaten and sun bleached, is symbolic of autumn for many reasons. Scarecrows represent the seasonal return to a slower

pace, a more casual look at life, and the happiness and joy that another productive rural summer can inspire. Scarecrows embody everything that we cherish about the change of seasons.

In this season of reflection and celebration, it is easy to forget how important scarecrows were during the busy working seasons on the farm. In the early spring when the earth is still damp and the air still carries a slight chill, the scarecrow is born. Fashioned from discarded objects and worn-out clothes, he is pieced together with a little of this and a little of that. The older and more patched the clothing, the better. The unwanted articles seem to glow as they begin their new life. A worn, flannel shirt stuffed with corn shocks allows the scarecrow to make a rustling sound when the wind blows. An old flour sack filled with newspaper serves as his face. Bit by bit, the scarecrow's uniform comes together, proudly adorning him in his working clothes. Perhaps the entire family creates

Anything goes when it comes to costuming a scarecrow. Using a flashy piece of clothing or finding a wonderful bit of flair is a great way to add a unique touch. Paulette Johnson

him, or it might be a child who pieces him together. Or maybe he is the handiwork of Grandmother, who finds joy in helping to do her share on the farm by creating this very special worker.

Then it is off to the fields or the garden, and the new scarecrow is propped up high on a wooden pole and left to stare out at the world with a huge grin. All through the months of the growing season, from the moment when the first seedlings pop their soft green leaves through the soil until the time when the ripened produce is harvested, the scarecrow stands sentinel over his domain, constantly keeping watch. The months of weather take their toll on the tireless worker. He is baked by the heat, hit by the rain, and burned by the wind for all of those months, and eventually his appearance reflects this. Yet it makes him even more of who he is; a scarecrow is characterized by the unruliness of his costume. As a farmer once said, "You can't make a scarecrow. He makes himself. In the

spring when you start to build him, he is just a tool; a tool for keeping critters away from the crops. But after you prop him up on that pole, well, then he's real."

Who made that first hero of the fields? Who was the first farmer who set out one day to create the perfect servant—the never-complaining, hard-working, inanimate, yet terribly authentic master of the fields? No one really knows for sure who created the first scarecrow, or even where the concept initially originated, but we do know that scarecrows have a long and entertaining history, spanning more than 3,000 years. They were initially created out of a genuine need to protect crops from being damaged by birds, which is a perennial problem that exists to this day. Hard-working farmers, intent on producing sufficient crops and gardens to nourish their families, could not spare the food destroyed by birds. Farmers worldwide have struggled with the problem of how to keep the birds away.

Historically, children were hired to patrol the farm fields as "bird scarers." These hard-working children were armed with rocks and were paid to chase away any birds that came near the fields. Farmers have also used scarecrows in various forms to scare away birds from their crops. In countries worldwide, these scarecrows have been known by such names as jack-of-straws, shoy-hoys, kakashis, scarebirds, tattybogles, mommets, murmets, vogelscheuchen, bootzamon, bootzafraus, and hodmedods. Some of the earliest scarecrows were those made by the ancient Egyptians, but Greek farmers also produced early scarecrows. The Greek scarecrows were made of wood and carved in the image of the Greek god Priapus, who was supposed to have been very ugly. The farmers believed that his face scared away the birds.

When the Pilgrims arrived in North America in the 1600s, they depended solely upon the crops they raised for survival. It was of utmost importance to protect their crops from being destroyed by birds or other creatures. Children were responsible for scaring away crows, deer, and wolves by running after them and scaring them away. In the 1700s and 1800s, people began creating scarecrows that are more reminiscent of the ones we use today. German immigrants used wooden frames and human clothing to create a *bootzamon* (bogeyman), and often created a female scarecrow to keep the bootzamon company. These female scarecrows were known as *bootzafraus* (bogeywife).

Interest in scarecrows lagged somewhat during the following years, but the coupled effects of the Great Depression and World War II prompted rejuvenated interest in gardening, and subsequently, rejuvenated interest in scarecrows.

Today, scarecrows are as important to the family garden or farm fields as they have ever been. Their primary purpose is guardian of the garden, but not all scarecrows are utilized in such diligent pursuits. Many scarecrows exist solely to give pleasure to their creators and perhaps to create a smile to someone passing by who spies the scarecrow relaxing on the front porch. These seasonal village inhabitants bring a spark of individuality to small-town and rural life and the chance for hard-working families to take a few moments to create something unique and entertaining. Scarecrows allow the expression of the artistic tastes

Making a scarecrow to decorate your yard is a great way to use clothes that are too far gone to repair. Daniel Johnson

Opposite:
Indian summer days are best spent outside. Making a scarecrow is a perfect way to spend one of the last few beautiful days in the sun. Daniel Johnson

Everyone must take time to sit and watch the leaves turn.
–Elizabeth Lawrence

Not all scarecrows stand at attention to ward off crows or other pests. This scarecrow is resting on the job.
Daniel Johnson

Opposite:
Creating a scarecrow is an activity for the entire family. It also is a way for children to let their creativity flow. This little fella is outfitting this scarecrow with a pumpkin.
Norvia Behling

of many individuals. Scarecrow making and decorating is an art—and one where the whole family and people of all ages can participate. Some people feel that there is no better way to spend a late summer afternoon than involved in the pursuit of creating a scarecrow, particularly because the possibilities and

opportunities for creative expression are limited only by the extent of one's imagination. Large or small, extravagant or simple, decorative scarecrows are a pleasure to the eye and a delight to behold.

Eccentricity is the hallmark of a scarecrow's appearance. Like snowflakes, each scarecrow is an individual and unlike any other. Contrary to popular belief, not all scarecrows wear patched overalls and flannel shirts stuffed with straw. Some scarecrows are fashioned from stacked pumpkins or adorned with reflective ribbon that blows in the wind, while others are created from broomsticks. Scarecrow faces are as unique as human faces and are made from a variety of objects: pumpkins, canvas, flour sacks, wood, pillowcases, milk jugs, and gourds.

Popular pursuits for scarecrow enthusiasts are annual scarecrow festivals all across the United States that celebrate the autumn season and the unique joy that scarecrows bring. One of the largest festivals is the St. Charles Scarecrow Festival (www.scarecrowfest.com), which is held over three days each October in St. Charles, Illinois. In addition to more than one hundred scarecrows on display, the festival also offers a flea market, petting zoo, carnival, haystack hunt, and other autumn fun for the entire family. Other annual scarecrow festivals are held in Wanatah, Indiana; Marshall, Michigan; and Bayfield, Wisconsin. Scarecrows are also a vital component of farms that are turning their attention toward the growing area of agritourism. While corn mazes and pumpkin patches are popular attractions for children who are visiting farms, scarecrows have a seemingly magnetic presence that draws visitors of all ages.

Part of the allure of scarecrows is that they are the culminating touch in a cast of harvest decorations. What else celebrates the season in quite the same way as a scarecrow? And yet, the scarecrow would not be quite complete if it was alone. Pumpkins, gourds, corn shocks, and Indian corn simply must accompany him. Nestled together with leaves and hay bales, these decorations truly epitomize the splendor of the season.

Scarecrows have their place in the world, all year long when utilized as a tool, but they are especially useful and whimsical during that incredible season on the farm: autumn. Like other beloved seasonal icons, such as Santa Claus or the Easter Bunny, scarecrows

have an interesting history and have evolved over time from their humble beginnings in ancient Egypt and Greece to their current status as farm helpers and autumn decorations. They evoke the feelings of a simpler lifestyle, a slower pace, and the joy of harvest time.

Even deeper still is the realization that scarecrows essentially represent all of the virtues and values of farm life. They represent diligence and a commitment to stick with a job until the task is completed. They represent a steadfast resolve to weather any storm that life presents, no matter how long or how difficult. Scarecrows represent thriftiness, the values of prudence and economy, and the adage of "waste not, want not." Scarecrows—like many who devote their time and energy to farming—couldn't possibly

be paid enough for their contributions of time and effort, yet they would undoubtedly refuse compensation if it was offered. The opportunity to witness the beauty of each and every day, coupled with ample time for pondering the joy of life, simply cannot have a monetary value assigned. Moreover, scarecrows, with their perennial smiling faces and whimsical approach to life, remind us all that finding joy in one's work is one of the deepest joys of all. Hard tasks are made easier when they are approached with a joyful heart.

And at the end of the day, when the sun fades and slips into an autumn sunset, the light fades from the fields until all that is left is the bit of light that is reflected on the face of that unconquerable worker, the scarecrow, staring out at the fields and knowing them all, silent and wise, the Solomon of the farm.

Two boys are busy shelling corn on a farm near Dublin, Georgia, in 1915. Library of Congress

Andrew Searles captured this photo of a raker at work on a Grand Rapids, Wisconsin, cranberry marsh in 1914. With a swinging motion, the prongs of the rake are thrust under the lowest layer of berries. The rake is pulled forward and up with the left hand to complete the arc. Each raker empties the berries into a box that is carried off by porters. Library of Congress

Opposite:
The bright, vividly colored leaves are a wonderful contrast to this straw-colored scarecrow. Daniel Johnson

A twelve-year-old boy tends to the chickens on his father's farm in Bennington, Vermont. Lewis W. Hine took this photo in August 1914. Library of Congress

The oak leaves turn gold during the crisp, clear days of October, the sunniest month of the year in the Midwest.
Lee Klancher

Harvesting What We Have Been Given

By Philip Hasheider

Combining his interests in dairy cattle, agriculture, and history, Philip Hasheider has written six books, including his most recent, How to Raise Cattle, *and numerous articles for national and international dairy breed publications. He was the recipient of the 2005 Book of Merit Award presented by the Wisconsin Historical Society and Wisconsin State Genealogical Society for* The Ancestry and Descendents of Alpheus & Sally (Copeland) Bass. *His diverse work has appeared in the Wisconsin Academy of Review, The Capital Times, Wisconsin State Journal, Sickle & Sheaf, Sauk Prairie Area Historical Society Newsletter, Sauk Prairie Eagle, Holstein World, and Nieuwsbrief, a publication based in the Netherlands.*

Philip currently resides near Sauk City, Wisconsin, with his wife and two children, who are all involved with the family's grass-fed beef farm. In this essay, Philip reflects upon fall and all of its life and creation. He also reminisces about his grandmother in this loving tribute to her and the beauty and nature of the autumn season.

Fall is the season of creation, not spring as many people think or would have us believe. Spring is simply the vehicle through which the seeds—that are harvested in the fall—take root. Fall is for gathering in these dormant buds that awaken with life on warm, wet spring days. Fall bears the fruits and is the base upon which life is built.

It is late in the year, but fall can arrive at its pleasure, elbowing its way into line between summer and winter. Fall steps into our lives on its own terms.

Fall is my favorite season on the farm because it is a time of thanksgiving and remembrance. The long, hot summer days are slowly cooling; the birds begin to gather for flight to distant places only they sense. The shadows grow shorter. The sun recedes quickly in the late afternoon, closing its shutters and stepping behind its curtain earlier each evening.

The roadside black-eyed Susans gently rock in the evening breeze, a breeze still mellow enough to leisurely watch the emerging stars without fear of being chilled. Cooing mourning doves gather on high wires, tucking in for the night. The quiet settles on the farmland like a soft, invisible blanket descending from the sky, hushing everything to stillness and sleep.

The fields of hay no longer wave; they have been cut short for harvest and stored for winter feeding.

The swooping swallows, once skimming the tops of blossoming brome grasses and mature timothy stalks and snatching bugs and insects for themselves, are no longer needed by their hatchlings, who have long since flown off on their own.

The days of harvest are beginning and are an annual reminder that but for a combination of sunlight, rain, and six inches of top soil, our existence is fragile. Everything else is frivolous: our cars, our social standing, and our technological gadgets. Without light, water, and soil, we would cease to exist.

Fall is a time to give thanks for these elements. It is a time to remember what and who made us: our families, our friends, our childhoods, and our choices. Fall is a time for review, the recounting of ourselves while we still have time and before the dark shadows of winter close in on our farms and our lives.

During fall there is time before winter arrives to bask in the light and look back over our shoulder at the months we hurried through, or across the long arc of many years and remember what we choose to.

Fall can sneak up on us, almost unnoticed. One day cool, another warm, the next day hot, as if summer struggles to hold its grip, unwilling to let go like an aging actor refusing to relinquish the glittering limelight of his youth, assisted off with a gentle but firm tug on the elbow by new, younger performers softly whispering in his ear that it's time to go. The next act has arrived, so just move on.

Fall is like that some years, lasting for months and lulling us with a false sense of security, its transition stretching endlessly as one warm day follows another, reminding us of summer's passion. Some years fall arrives one day and vanishes the next without the slightest protest, like a guest who quickly leaves because he or she remembers something more important to do.

Fall doesn't confront you like winter, forcing you to bend to its will. Winter can slap you with cold, icy fingers only moments after you thought the worst was past. It resurrects itself when least expected. Fall lets you linger, lets you dream, and lets you wonder. It allows you to lie on the ground, look up at the stars, and believe in the purpose of their existence and yours. Fall is a time for imagination. Winter will have none of that and forces you back to reality and basic survival.

Fall does not watch a calendar. Green leaves sway on borrowed time, stealing extra moments in the breeze and sun and cheating their own death as they cling to the branches, oblivious to the inevitable. On a crisp, clear fall day, nature draws us in, clutching us to keep warm like embers in a dying fire, fearful of losing us to winter.

Fall pushes us out of our stagnant selves and inspires us to dream of things to come. Fall prompts us to create circumstances of our own making and design rather than succumbing to what simply comes our way. Fall is the time of creation.

But fall is also an end—the end of growing before the harvest, the end of life in the maturing fields when they reveal themselves as the finished promises of spring.

I thought about these things as I sat waiting for the combine to eject its heavy load of corn into my empty wagon, the open-air tractor sitting at the north end of the long-rowed field. I had time to watch the hour pass and observe the mammoth mechanical harvester race from one end of the field to the other, gobbling up the stalks, shelling off kernels, and disgorging all the refuse—the broken and crimpled stalks, empty crushed cobs, and billowing chaff—out the rear and onto the dry ground.

The fields are awash with bounty, the corn ears full and plump. At an earlier time, they were ripped from their stalks by men and boys in leathered gloves,

who quickly worked up and down the standing rows, throwing each kernel-laced cob into the horse-drawn wagon, filling it as they went.

Those days are mostly gone. Some say good riddance as huge machines with insatiable appetites continue to run as long as someone is willing to sit in the warm cab and drive across the fields to satisfy the

*The first signs of fall are visible in the changing leaves on
the trees near this weathered Wisconsin barn.*
Catnap, shutterstock

A 60-horsepower Caterpillar-engine combine harvester was used in the Deschutes Valley in central Oregon. Harvesting was a big job, so many neighbors would travel from farm to farm to help each other out. This photograph was taken on September 3, 1912, by O. Hedlund. Library of Congress

Real "horse power" propelled this combine harvester through the golden grain fields of California in 1902. Library of Congress

Pumpkin patches pop up all over the countryside when the leaves start to turn. Many people from the area and neighboring towns come to the pumpkin patch to spend a beautiful fall day on the farm. Daniel Johnson

addiction to keep moving. The methods of harvest may have changed, but it is still the same harvest of generations past.

Was it always like this—the speed and impatience? Not as I remember it. The time of harvests past was always busy, but there was time for appreciation brought on by a slower pace that was measured in days, not hours. The harvest now is treated as a commodity for the highest market or bidder—stored, then sold. It is often destined for far away places and people who have never seen the land stretching out before me.

It was a commodity years ago, but it was more than a product to be sold. It was the food of life for the entire farm, the animals, and for the family. Oats and hay were grown for the horses that provided the power to propel the machines. Horses had to stop for rest and water and could not run for ten hours at a time like machines today. Farmers had to stop and bide their time because their horses needed to rest.

The entire crop was used. Corn husks, cobs, and stalks were fed to the pigs who provided the pork—the bacon and hams for the family—and the lard for cooking and baking. Corn and seeds were fed to the chickens that laid the eggs used for baking or frying in a pan on a woodstove at breakfast time. Oats were fed to horses, chickens, and pigs and the straw was used for bedding under the cows, in the heifer stalls, and in the pig sty. When the stalls and pens were cleaned out, the solid and packed manure was hauled onto fields to be worked back into the soil as food for the next year's crops. It fed the soil, which fed the plants, which fed the animals, which fed the family. Fall was for recycling, and farmers made the most of it.

Fall is for remembering June's explosion of peony blossoms circling the lawn and of lilacs swaying in the May breeze with their blossoms' lavender fragrance wafting in the air swirling around the house. Some years, when they bloomed for a week, they seemed to last forever.

A trip down the lane to a back pasture on a brisk fall morning doesn't seem like much of a chore when the scenery is this beautiful. Puchan, shutterstock

I cannot endure to waste anything as precious as autumn sunshine by staying in the house. So I spend almost all the daylight hours in the open air.
–Nathaniel Hawthorne

My grandmother loved these lingering fall days. I remember a time one spring when she was standing near her lilac bushes, her nose turned toward the breeze, and her eyes shut. She just stood there, breathing in their presence, her slight shoulders gently rising and falling as she drew in their fragrance, holding it ever so slightly, and then slowly releasing her breath.

For her, the world stopped; the dinner dishes could wait, the ironing would be there later, and the clothes would be hung soon. It all could wait as she stood for what seemed like an hour but was only minutes.

I've often wondered what she was thinking because I could see a gentle smile creep around the corners of her mouth, perhaps remembering. But remembering what? Was it the time her new husband cut off little lilac sprigs with his pocket knife and brought her a small bouquet that first spring after they were married? Or was she remembering when her tiny daughter, holding a handful of crushed blossoms, came toddling into her outstretched arms, offering them as a precious gift, which she took and later pressed into her favorite book to remember that moment years later?

Or maybe she was remembering her own childhood friends who used to play amongst the lilac bushes at school during their noon break, so many of them no longer with her in the fall of her life.

She finally turned and sensing my bewilderment, simply said, "Oh, if only I could bottle that smell and stop it up with a cork, I'd have it for the rest of the year. Smelling them in the middle of winter would simply be heaven."

After that morning, I can't smell lilacs without thinking of my grandmother standing by those bushes. She is permanent to that time and spot, sketched with indelible ink, never fading. Was she thinking of my grandfather then? Was that how she kept him to herself since he's been gone?

Where do our memories finally go when we can no longer remember? Are they locked away in some cosmological drawer waiting to be opened in some future existence? Will those memories simply transport us back to where we started, melding us with our past to become, once again, our future? Will our lives start over again?

What will happen to my memories when I'm gone? Will my memory of my grandmother standing there breathing in the blooming lilacs simply be lost to all eternity? Will they continue to lie dormant in my silent brain, long after I'm dead, only to be reawakened on some distant shore of eternity? Perhaps that's what memories are for.

My grandmother liked those lingering fall days when they stayed warm and the evenings held a slight chill. She loved walking around her backyard, needing neither overcoat nor the black shawl that often draped her shoulders to keep the chill away. She seemed free of those encumbrances as she walked back to her apple tree, the soft breeze dancing around her, flicking the loose gray wisps of her hair about her head.

She carried her small wicker basket in the crook of her slender arm and stood erect as she picked ripe apples from the tree. She picked these first and left the windfalls for later when she would examine them. Those still good enough to use would go for baking, and those past salvaging would go to her son's farm and be tossed to the fattening hogs.

My grandmother would make the good apples into pies or dry slices for supper treats. I remember being in her kitchen when she would peel the apple skins with her sharp paring knife, quickly and deftly rotating the apple as she sliced in one continuous peel until she got to the bottom. Then with one quick flick of her wrist, she severed the peel from the apple and dropped it into the porcelain dish sitting on her white-aproned lap.

Then she carved the slices, like one whittling away a piece of wood, until she reached the core. I quietly watched her, often wondering, maybe even marveling, how she kept from slicing off her fingers. I would have lost three by then. She finished all the apples and put the cores and browning peels into a bucket to go to the farm.

For a woman who accomplished so much and worked so hard, her hands seemed remarkably soft—not like my grandfather's, with thick, leathery calluses on his hands and fingers, the result of years of heavy farm work, long before modern machines eased his efforts. The lifting, pounding, and hand-milking all had left their imprint which no knife could seem to penetrate or cut open.

My grandmother had kneaded the dough for the crust hours before and after taking it from the refrigerator, she rolled it out on the counter with a wooden rolling pin. She created her dough and never measured anything out. She simply used her eye to measure and instinctively knew when there was enough of each ingredient.

Laying the crust over the pie pan, she gently pressed it down with her fingers and, after smoothing out the wrinkles, cut around the pan with her knife and sliced off dough that crept over the edge. Spreading the apple slices in the pan, she lightly sprinkled cinnamon and brown sugar over them and laid a second layer of dough over the top. Placing it into the hot oven, she closed the door and went into her parlor to finish some mending.

She was alone in the house, except for me. I can't recall the number of times I was there. While my grandfather was alive, he and I would sit in anticipation until the oven opened and she brought out her finished pie or hickory nut cookies. It now was quiet in her house, with only the sound of her old clock ticking away the minutes, breaking the silence as she sat alone in the other room.

It was in the fall of the year when my grandmother died. They said it was a sudden passing like so many others, as if you could think thousands of people dying in the same way as being similar, collective deaths instead of individuals.

Hers was not a lingering illness. One sunny, warm, fall day—the kind she loved so well—she was working on her rose bush, snipping away dead branches and collecting little flowers, those that still lingered, clutching to their own lives. She placed them in a glass bowl on her kitchen table to better see them when she ate her meals alone.

She didn't like living alone. Although the eight months since my grandfather's death shouldn't have seemed that long, she said soon after his passing that the days seemed awfully long without him. He had passed through the fall of his life and reached his winter, having left her behind through no fault of his own. But sometimes her anger at him arose for going on ahead without her.

She was found the next morning when her daughter came over to see if something was wrong

A rainbow of apples shine in the autumn sunshine. Apple orchards in the fall are fragrant with the trees heavy with crisp, ripe apples. Daniel Johnson

Opposite:
This girl has found her perfect pumpkin. An autumn tradition for many is heading to the pumpkin patch in search of the perfect pumpkin to carve into a jack-o-lantern that will be proudly displayed on the porch. Daniel Johnson

because she failed to place her routine phone call at precisely the same hour each morning. Her son was called. He came to the house without changing his barn clothes and together they looked at their mother lying on the bed, sleeping as they thought she must always have slept since their father was gone, facing his empty pillow, her left arm resting on her hip.

My grandmother never wore her wedding ring to bed. She always placed it on a lace towel that was embroidered by her mother with little pink rose

petals, which was given as a wedding present sixty years before.

But on this night, of all the nights over those sixty years, she slipped her wedding ring back onto her finger as she made herself ready for bed. She must have brushed her hair before retiring for they found her brushes lying at the foot of the bed. Two soft hair brushes sitting side by side, as if placed there gently with purpose.

Had she known what lay ahead? Did she sense this night would be different from all others? Was she preparing herself once more for her wedding day, a bride of spring taking the hand of the man she loved and lived with for those many years, walking forward with him again, into her future, trusting whatever it may bring? I would like to think so; that deep within our psyche, we can connect with those we love but who have departed. It makes understanding life so much easier.

That's why I like fall, because you can assess your life, on your own terms, while there still is time—time to remember and reclaim those who touched our lives and made us who we are.

You can have spring with its promises or summer with its potential. But I'll take fall when all promises and potential meld together into one season of beautiful fulfillment. Fall is a time for release and of letting go what we cannot hold. There is no shame in realizing we cannot stand against time's silent clock, slowly, steadily ticking away beyond our hearing but not our sensing.

We see time's effects: the ripening wheat, the swaying fields of hay, the golden tassels of corn, our graying hair, and our dying friends. Time marches on, and we must stay in step or be left behind. There is no alternative. Winter lies ahead.

Rejoice in fall while it is still with us. Bathe in the glory of its bountiful harvest; it is what sustains us, implores us, and confirms us. With fall's cartwheeling leaves dancing through yards and rustling grasses laughing again, take to the paths and walk with the season and remember family and friends. In fall, all things are possible: reaping, sowing, planting, harvesting, growing, and remembering.

If I close my eyes on a warm fall day, I can, for just a moment, become a child again. I can see my grandmother standing over her woodstove oven, her back

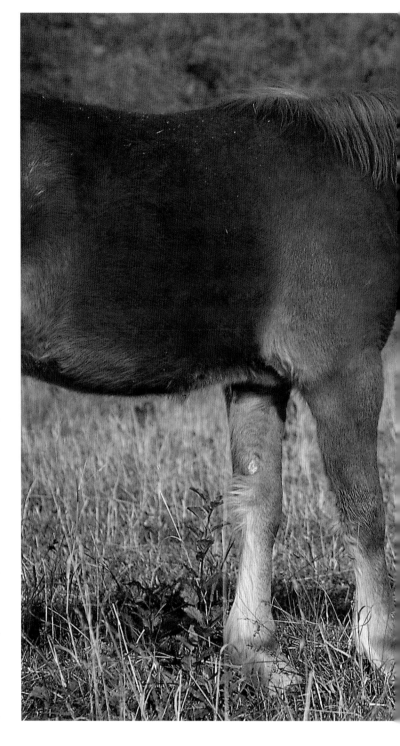

toward the table, and my grandfather sitting camouflaged behind a newspaper.

It's quiet again except for the slight humming she's making, standing and timing the baking in her mind and not by a clock. Before long, the smell of sweet cinnamon rises from the oven, drifting across the room, and my grandfather tips his paper to look over. Steam rises from the plate as she cradles the pan between her hands covered with heavy cloth mittens.

October's poplars are flaming torches
lighting the way to winter.
–Nova Bair

Sunny fall days are best spent outside with your animals. You never know when winter will make its harsh appearance so it's best to take advantage of beautiful weather when you can. Daniel Johnson

First John Deere Combine Delivered - May-18-1928 - To Charley - Fred Janne

The note on the bottom of this archival photograph states that this was the first John Deere combine delivered with a date of May 18, 1928.

Opposite:
Milkweed pods dry up and break open during the fall. Their feathery seeds are blown along the countryside by the cool autumn winds. Lee Klancher

With my eyes closed, I can take a deep breath and be transported back in time. My shoulders rising and falling with a rhythm not unlike my grandmother's when smelling the lilacs. I sense the sweet cinnamon filling the room, and time is unable to douse that smell drifting across the years.

I can see my grandfather setting down his newspaper and taking an interest as we watch her place the dish on a wooden rack in the middle of the kitchen table. She gently places a wide slice before me on a small plate. She gives me a fork, and in my mind, I'm lifting a piece and slowly raising it to my mouth.

If I could just bottle that smell, then I could keep it forever. But my eyes come open, and she evaporates before me; I'm standing beside her lilac bush. It's fall now for me, and it's been a long time since I've tasted one of her apple pies.

The Ghosts of Middle Mound

By Lee Klancher

November in Wisconsin is as distinctive as any season on the farm, as the woods crawl with neon-orange-clad hunters pursuing one of the state's favorite game animals, the whitetail deer. Lee Klancher returns to his family land near Willard, Wisconsin, each year to join in the hunt, an annual ritual that his family has participated in since hunters were first required to buy one-dollar tags to hunt back in 1897. During a November 2006 hunt through his favorite section of woods, Lee chronicles the memories housed in the hills and concludes that deer hunting each November is more than just a sport—it's a measure of time.

When I hunt on my family's land in central Wisconsin each November, I'm shadowed by tall oaks that were sprouting from acorns when my Slovenian great-grandfather Frank Klanchar (the family later Americanized the name by changing the spelling to Klancher) packed up his wife, Frances, and left Ely, Minnesota, to come to Willard, Wisconsin. Hunting season is my time to spend some time with the land, a piece of ground rich with history. The nooks and crannies of our land are as crowded with memories as the Lambeau Field parking lot before a playoff game.

As Frank cut down trees to clear fields to feed his growing family, the oaks on Middle Mound grew to be saplings. My grandfather, Paul Senior, was born in 1914 into Frank's family of nine and was a rambunctious part of his small Slovenian community in central Wisconsin. He was blowing up milk cans with stolen dynamite (a prank that left him deaf for a week), while the oaks on Middle Mound stretched into young trees.

In the 1960s, after my father, Paul Junior, got married and took a job as a middle school math teacher in a small town several hours north of Willard, my grandfather bought a place on Middle Mound, and he and Frieda, my grandmother, built a house. I was born, Frank and Frances passed away, and the saplings had

Lee Klancher shot his first buck in November 1980. Here he poses with his deer and his grandfather, Paul Senior.
Frieda Klancher

Phil and Jennifer (Wheeler) Sedlack pause for a photo on the Klancher-Wheeler family's hunting land in central Wisconsin.
Lee Klancher

become large enough to shelter the squirrels, grouse, and deer Dad and Grandpa hunted on the mound.

On a thirty-degree day in November 2006, I'm standing at the bottom of the south face of Middle Mound looking up on this stand of century-old oak trees. This is my twenty-eighth year hunting the hill, and it is one of my favorite places on our land. By the time deer hunting season rolls around in late November, the trees are stripped bare and the leaves blanket the face of the hill in an ankle-deep carpet. I enjoy the company of those stately old trees even when the winds of November turn cold and the carpet of leaves is coated white with snow.

We drive Middle Mound every year, and I always take the route that crosses the south face. That route is the most difficult physically but potentially the most rewarding, as bucks have an affinity for lying among the oaks on the south face. I've never shot a buck on this drive, but I continue to make the trek up the south face in the hope that I will. I also make the drive purely for the sake of history. Walking the south face is a tradition, another piece of the annual celebration that is deer hunting season.

On the Saturday after Thanksgiving, the second-to-last day of the 2006 rifle season, I'm standing at the base of the south face watching my old friend Jennifer Sedlack, her husband, Phil, and their four-year-old son, Dillon, walk up the hill. The drive consists of six of us strung out in a line to making our way across the mile-long hill known as Middle Mound. Five members of our hunting party are waiting on the other end of the hill in the hope that we'll drive some deer past them.

Jennifer is taking her traditional route, which is walking the top of the ridge above the south face. Dillon is following her on his first hunting outing. Jennifer is not carrying a gun on this drive so that she can focus on Dillon. The pair's role is to coordinate the drivers on both sides of the hill. She can see me on the south face and, to the north, she can see into a valley known as the Bowl, an oak- and pine-filled hollow in the center of Middle Mound that the other members of the drive will pass through on the drive.

Once Jennifer reaches the top, she takes a minute to catch her breath. Phil continues on down into the Bowl. Under Jennifer's watch from the top of the hill, all of the drivers—Phil included—take their places.

Across the Bowl and over a series of hardwood-covered humps, a weathered, old fence post marks four intersecting property lines. In the fall of 1984, my grandfather shot his last buck only a few yards from that post. He wounded it with his crossbow, and my dad and Grandpa's faithful beagle, Feastus, were called in to track and kill the wounded deer.

Grandpa's gone now, taken by a heart attack in February 1985. We tell stories about his escapades often, as he was the steward of our deer hunting land for most of his life. A bit of an outlaw who loved hunting and his grandkids, his presence on the hunting land is felt in the roads he cut, stands he built, and stories of him that are told and retold.

Jennifer looks across this valley to see when Dad has the rest of his crew in place on the other side of the Bowl. Once they are, she waves down to me, and we start the drive.

I make my way across the sliding hill, across a game path that threads through a tangle of blackberry briars and into the woods. The steep, rocky hill is covered in a thick carpet of oak leaves that make for slick footing.

I move slowly through this area, both because crossing this section of woods is hard work, and because my dad taught me when I was young to move slowly and to stop often when hunting. When you stop, animals get nervous and jump.

Dad also taught me to know how to shoot well and, when the time comes, take care and shoot once. When I was eighteen I missed my first buck, a beauty of a six-pointer that ran past me in the shade of another stand of oaks on my grandfather's land across from the mound. After emptying my gun at the deer in vain, Dad's advice took. By the time I was nineteen, I had adopted his wisdom as my own.

But in order to shoot, you have to find the deer, and I'm not doing that on this crystal clear November day. I'm not particularly disturbed by this fact. The sun is warm on the south face, and I pause to draw deep breaths of the oak-leaf-scented air.

The deer crew gathers to discuss the morning hunt in the pines on the foot of Middle Mound near Willard, Wisconsin.
Lee Klancher

More than ten years ago, on a snowy November afternoon, I stopped and listened close to this same spot and was rewarded with the crackling of leaves that indicated a group of animals moving through the woods. I saw a long line of dark shapes moving through the brush about one hundred yards ahead—ten or maybe twelve of them. I excitedly put up my rifle to scope the group, hopeful the long line contained a buck.

The shapes in the scope were pearlike, a Seussical joke of an animal. It took a few seconds for me to realize that these were not deer but wild turkeys, crashing along through the snow-crusted oak leaves and over the hill. We did not have turkeys in our woods during my formative years. The DNR planted them in our area in the late 1980s, and in a few years, the turkeys returned. That snowy day was the first time I saw them in the woods.

Today, all I hear when I stop is the sound of Jennifer and Dillon crunching along on the top of the mound. The top of the hill is a good spot for bow hunting, and I shot a little doe up there more than a decade ago. I didn't place the arrow well, and she took too long to die. That was the last deer I shot with a bow.

I move on across the hill and come to a fence line about a quarter-mile into the woods. At the fence line, I stop and wait for Jennifer to call from the top of the hill. We traditionally wait there and get the entire crew lined up. Staying lined up is a key to a successful drive, as important as Dad's stop, look, and listen rule.

She calls out, I respond, and we move on. The section of the woods after the fence is not nearly as steep and opens up a bit. The walking is easier, and I am treated to an expansive view of the hollow ahead. At the bottom of the hollow is a little knoll where Dad and I built a stand for my now ex-wife, Renee.

Renee once stood in that stand while fifteen does came past, but she never pulled the trigger. She took a lot of guff for not firing, but Renee was as tough as she was cautious. She shot a nice little buck a year later, dropped with a single shot at ninety yards. When her time came to make a shot, she did so precisely. That was Renee.

Just up the hill from that spot, Dad later built a tree stand that has become his favorite on opening morning. He shot the biggest buck taken in camp from that stand, and still consistently sees bucks from this vantage point.

Across this valley and on top of the hill is a spot known as the Saddle, and it is a favorite place to stand. Jennifer's then-boyfriend now-husband, Phil, stood there his second year of hunting, and a buck stood in front of him, down the hill enough so all Phil could see was his rack of antlers. That buck escaped, but Phil shot another one near there a few years later that is one of the largest ever taken at camp.

My dad had given Phil directions for how to find the Saddle a few years back and told him, "Walk the top of the mound until you see a tree, then turn right."

The top of the mound is covered with trees, hundreds of them, so Dad's directions were hard for Phil to decipher. Dad's line has become a catch phrase and is used as a joke nearly every time someone gives directions at deer camp.

The line may have been humorous, but I knew exactly which tree Dad was talking about: a gnarled, old oak standing tall at the top of the ridge, not far from the fox's den. If you spend enough time in a place, the topography makes an imprint on your soul. The haunts and hollows of the land becomes a guidebook to your life.

The last part of the drive goes through a swampy stand of poplars next to the old spring in the hollow below the Saddle. Deer often lay near the spring, and this is the part of the drive where I most often see them running through the woods.

I creep through the woods and the hill, and I glimpse two does running ahead of me. I scope them as they run, but the shot is not a good one. We have plenty of meat in the freezer, and I don't want to force a poor shot

and risk wounding a deer and spending the afternoon tracking. I watch as they run away, their long white tails flagging their progress until they disappear over the rise.

I walk over the hill and emerge from the woods in the small clearing next to a 400-yard-wide stand of thick pines. The pines were planted by my grandfather in the early 1970s, and they've grown to become a safe haven for deer. The deer that made it into those pines today have survived our efforts. The drive is over.

Several of our members shot does and are visible on the hillside, orange jackets hanging on a tree limb as they dress the deer. The Mickelsen boys are energetically hiking out to get a four-wheeler to retrieve the animals.

The hunt is done, but the best part of the drive remains as we gather in blaze orange circles to find out who shot, who missed, and the other events that make each drive an event.

This year, the story is my uncle Pat's new stand on the Turkey Knob. He brought an old, overstuffed recliner into the woods and placed it at the base of a tree. When he sits in his stand on the Turkey Knob, he does so in style.

Some of the best jokes of the year are told in these circles. Good jokes have history and context. Like Dad's "When you see a tree" line, most of the jokes told in the woods during deer camp have multiple layers of meaning.

A few minutes later, called by the growl of my stomach, I decide to head in for lunch. Crossing the fence in a hollow about 150 yards from my aunt and uncle's cabin, I stop and remember my close friend Dave Linner's first buck. It ran past him in our land across the road from the mound, and he shot. He said it was a "monster," a giant buck that ran past him. He thought he had hit it, so he recruited help tracking the animal.

The buck, a nice little six-pointer, was found dead only a few feet from where I now stood. It wasn't a monster, but it was Dave's first buck. He was proud as could be, and I helped him drag the deer out and load it into my truck to register it.

Dave was a flight medic and became the director of the Yampa Valley Air Ambulance in Hayden, Colorado. A few years after he shot his first buck, he was on a plane flying into Casper, Wyoming, to pick up a young girl in dire straits. The plane iced up and went down, taking Dave with it.

We have a photo of him, hanging next to some trinkets that commemorate his pranks, up in the guys' room in one of the sheds.

Dave was only at our deer camp a few times, but his antics have become camp legend. The world is a little quieter without him, and his absence hangs heavily on this somber little piece of Middle Mound.

The Sedlack family shakes me from my reveries by noisily making their way out of the woods a few yards ahead of me. Dillon is excitedly telling (and retelling) about the turkeys he saw during his walk with his mom.

"Did you know I saw turkeys, Dad? They were huge!"

I hurry to catch up and hear the rest of Dillon's story. The four of us head in for some of my Aunt Kay's clam chowder. The earthy soup is bubbling hot and thick on the stove, ready to warm the blood of hunters coming in for lunch. The cabin is bathed in the afternoon sunshine pouring in the windows and full of kids shooting Nerf rockets from the loft, adults packed around Kay's table eating soup, and others sprawled on the couches taking naps or catching a bit of football before heading out for the afternoon hunt.

David Linner (1968–2005) on the front side of Middle Mound. Lee Klancher

On the south face of Middle Mound, the oaks are also basking in the afternoon sun. Deer hunting season is almost over, and a long winter awaits. But spring will arrive to clear the south face of snow. The sunshine will coax a fresh crop of buds from those trees and turn the hillside green in the heat of summer. The oak leaves will paint the hill burnt gold and orange in the October sun and be blown to earth by the cold winds of November.

The oaks won't be alone. As long as I'm able, I'll hunt in the shadows of those old trees to make my annual pilgrimage to visit the ghosts of Middle Mound.

*August, Mary, Tina, Saraphina, Jennie, and Edgar Kruegar are pictured husking corn on their Wisconsin
farm. Harvesting corn was a task for the entire family before the convenience of a corn shredder and picker.*
Wisconsin Historical Society

HARVEST SUPPERS

By Carolyn Lumsden

Carolyn Lumsden didn't grow up on a farm but learned about farm life the hard way: as a farm wife. Carolyn and her husband, Gary, raised hogs and beef cattle and maintained a dairy herd on their farm in northwest Wisconsin. Carolyn has written many humorous essays about the lessons she has learned on the farm and how nature affects all those who live in the country. Her stories have appeared in many publications, including Country Woman, Wisconsin Agriculturist, *and* Farm Woman News.

There are many rural traditions, and a very popular one that occurs in the fall is the annual harvest supper. It is a chance for the neighborhood to gather and give thanks for the growing season. It's also a chance for neighbors to sit and visit and catch up on each other's lives after a busy summer of work.

Harvest time is an important time in any farming community. Our homemakers' group consisted of many farm women or women who came from farm backgrounds. One important and fun yearly activity was our annual harvest supper.

After the date was chosen, we started planning the neighborhood festivities. A local, former two-room schoolhouse was the location. The schoolhouse had been converted into a community center and was maintained by our homemakers' group members and their husbands. An integral part of our neighborhood, the schoolhouse was the site of many functions, such as wedding showers, card games, plays, quilting bees, flower shows, family reunions, and the annual harvest supper.

The harvest supper was scheduled to begin after the evening milking chores, which was around 8:00 p.m. Farm families would hurry and finish their chores so that everyone could attend. Neighbors and friends came from all around to share the harvest meal and camaraderie.

In one of the large rooms, kitchen cabinets, donated by someone who had remodeled her kitchen, had been installed. These held the many dishes and other supplies we had accumulated through the years. Few items matched, but no one seemed to care. Several large, blue enamel coffee pots had also been donated. An electric range had been installed for brewing the large enameled pots of coffee, keeping foods hot in the oven, and some light cooking. There wasn't indoor plumbing in the building because the school wasn't heated over the winter, so the stove also heated the water for washing dishes. A sink was installed, and the drain was piped outside.

When the hand pump outside the building was working, we used the water from that pump. If for some reason the pump was inoperable, usually because someone had accidentally backed into it, several milk cans of water were brought from a local farm for cleanup after the supper.

With no running water, it's quite obvious that the restroom facilities consisted of two drafty outhouses out back. In the kitchen, a sturdy twenty-foot serving counter had been built by the neighborhood men. They also built long, sturdy, rustic tables that were covered with tablecloths for events. A couple of large, round, oak tables had also been donated and supplied more room to eat. Mismatching wooden chairs provided a place for people to sit for the many events held at the schoolhouse. Harvest suppers were wonderful celebrations, symbolized by the bounty of food. Every family brought a dish to pass. There were smokehouse-cured hams, farm-fattened beef roasts and meatballs, free-roam chicken prepared in several ways, casseroles of many kinds, garden fresh vegetables and salads, and homemade breads and buns. Desserts were made from scratch and included cakes, pumpkin and apple pies, bars, cookies, and gelatins

Deer hunting is an annual fall tradition for many families. Every hunter pines for a big buck, but the main purpose of deer hunting is to put venison in the freezer. This is the Glaser and Eliason hunting crew outside of Bill and Mildred Glaser's farm, circa mid-1950s.
Courtesy of Kenneth and Shirley Glaser

Group suppers were a great place to catch up with your family and neighbors after the busy summer season on the farm. Everyone brought a dish to pass, and no one ever went away hungry.

with farm-fresh whipped cream to tempt everyone. Laden with food, the long serving counter contained plenty for second helpings. No one worried about calories that night.

When the food and egg-coffee (raw eggs and eggshells are added to the grounds), made by Scandinavian women, were ready, it was time to eat. A thanksgiving prayer was said, and soon the neighbors lined up to begin piling their plates with the numerous food selections.

Often the crowd was too large for seating in the one room, and people spilled into the second schoolroom, in search of any place they could sit and eat. Kids often sat on the floor of the stage area in the second schoolroom.

People visited with each other as they ate. Neighborhood news was shared. There was talk about harvesting problems and yields, the weather, family news, or changes in the local towns.

To entertain the children, we'd plan fun activities to keep them occupied. A very popular activity was the fish pond. Neighborhood women donated the prizes for the fish pond. The items varied from toys no longer used by their children to candy, games, puzzles, and handknit or crocheted mitts, scarves, or stuffed animals. White sheets were hung from the ceiling

around a table full of the donated items. One person would stand outside the "pond" and help the child with a cane fishing pole. The fishing line would be tossed over the top of the sheet and another person inside the sheet area would tie a surprise onto the line. With a slight tug to indicate when the child had caught the "fish," the line would be lifted over the sheet and the child received a surprise on the end of his or her line. Because it was such a close-knit community, everyone knew the children, and often a clue would be given to the person behind the sheet to help select a gift for the child.

Another popular activity was fortunetelling. I was asked to be the fortuneteller, and after pondering for some time and doing some research at the local library, I decided to read palms. I memorized the various

These farmers used both types of horsepower (in this case, mule power) to harvest corn in this vintage John Deere advertisement.

The barn door that stood wide open all summer long now has to be shut to keep the cold autumn air out at night. But there is a feeling of satisfaction when you close the door on a snug barn full of animals and a year's supply of hay in the haymow. Daniel Johnson

Opposite:
This old shed was a favorite of Paul C. Klancher, who spent many hours out there tinkering with traps, old motors, and fishing lures. He built a larger steel shed, and this one became a storage place. Lee Klancher

lines on the hand and what those lines should mean. My "fortunes" were based on those meanings, such as a long life, meeting someone wonderful to marry, or taking a long trip.

My fortunetelling became a bit more sophisticated thanks to a few props. When taking a load of unwanted items to our local dump (there were no recycling facilities back then), I found a round, clear glass globe about six inches in diameter with a black base. In years past it was a decoration and held an artificial red rose. I removed the faded rose and put in a few strands of white angel hair to make it look like wisps of smoke.

To look like a stereotypical gypsy, I wore a red, printed, flared skirt with a matching head scarf, several bracelets, and dangling, gold earrings. Bright red lipstick and matching red fingernails completed my mystical transformation.

I made up a few fortunes that could happen to anyone as I peered into my "crystal ball." Some examples were: You'll meet someone you haven't seen in a while. You'll receive something unexpected next week. You and your brother/sister will have a disagreement. You'll

go on a short trip within a month. These fortunes were ordinary things a child would do.

In my research, I stumbled upon an interesting invisible writing trick. I cut pieces of paper and wrote fortunes on the paper with lemon juice. Once the juice was dry, the writing was not visible. I put the fortunes into a box and let each child select a "blank" piece of paper. I would hold the paper over a burning candle, and brown writing would magically appear. The children's eyes would widen and stare at the

The corn has been harvested, and the silos on the farm are full. A successful harvest will feed the farm's livestock through the long, cold winter. A field full of cornstalks is a wonderful sight to a farmer. John Wollwerth, shutterstock

This young girl doesn't mind her chores at all. Taking care of her horses is something that she looks forward to every day. Daniel Johnson

The wind that makes music in November corn is in a hurry. The stalks hum, the loose husks whisk skyward in half-playing swirls, and the wind hurries on. A tree tries to argue, bare limbs waving, but there is no detaining the wind.
–Aldo Leopold

paper as I read their fortunes before I gave them the piece of paper. They were enthralled with that trick.

One time when I was telling a fortune to a child, I overheard two children talking. "I KNOW she's a REAL gypsy. She can read blank pieces of paper. I picked out a piece of paper, and she held it over a candle. Writing appeared. Honest!" I tried not to smile but didn't succeed. Dark brown eyes of the young boy I was telling a fortune to stared at me. I quickly made up a fun fortune, and then he smiled too.

Another popular activity with children and adults was the cake walk. One of our talented homemakers played the old upright piano that was sometimes out of tune. Squares were made on the floor with chalk, or pieces of paper were taped onto the floor. Each square had a number. When the piano was being played, people walked in a circle formed by the squares on the floor. When the music quit, a number was drawn. The person standing on that number won a donated cake made by the neighborhood women. Whoever won a cake was delighted to take a wonderful, homemade cake home.

The adults enjoyed camaraderie as the children were entertained. After a leisurely meal and a lot of visiting and storytelling, the cleanup committee began to gather the dishes. Often the older girls would help with this task. The women on the cleanup committee and some of the older girls washed, wiped, and put away the dishes. As they cleaned up, they shared news of family and the community. When they were finished, tablecloths and wet dishtowels were folded and were taken home to be laundered.

Like all get-togethers, one by one families gathered their empty food containers and tired children, and left for their homes. Farm chores would have to be done in the morning once again.

Usually two families lingered to sweep the floors, rearrange the chairs, and set things back in order. The lights were shut off, the door closed, and another successful, happy, and rewarding harvest supper with neighbors and friends of our farming community had ended for another year.

A barn cat is always keeping a watchful eye on its farm. Maybe it's looking for field mice that are scurrying to find a warm home for the winter. Samantha Johnson

These Australian shepherds are running and playing among the round bales. On beautiful, warm fall days everyone wants to soak in the sun, including the dogs! Shirley Fernandez

The early morning fog that hasn't burned off casts a mysterious aura on this autumn morning. The cool, autumn air sparks creative minds and is the perfect setting for spooky ghost stories. Michal Rozanski, shutterstock

CHAPTER 4

Winter

*Winter is the time for comfort, for good food and
warmth, for the touch of a friendly hand, and for
a talk beside the fire: it is the time for home.*
–Dame Edith Sitwell

Winter settles in and covers the farm in a blanket of cold and
snow. The fields hibernate to rest up for the new growing
season in the spring. The animals huddle together for warmth and
dot the landscape like wooly mammoths, plump and covered in
thick, winter coats of fur. The crunch of snow underfoot as you
trudge to the barn is a peaceful sound in the dark stillness of the
morning. A deep breath of the biting wind awakens the mind and
grants a moment of clarity that can only be created by the clean
winter air. The cold weather can be brutal at times, but we forge
ahead because work still needs to be done.

*Postcards were a very popular
way of corresponding in the late
1800s and early 1900s. Christmas
postcards were a perfect way to
send a bit of holiday cheer to family
and friends.*

Opposite:
*The sun rises over an abandoned
farm near Greenwood, Wisconsin.*
Lee Klancher

Horses kick up their heels on a snowy morning. Daniel Johnson

FEEDING THE CRITTERS

By Gwen Petersen

Gwen Petersen's early work as a registered occupational therapist in psychiatric hospitals for the bothered and bewildered helped her prepare for her later career as a ranch wife. She lives with her husband on a small ranch near Big Timber, Montana, along with an assortment of cattle, pigs, sheep, chickens, cats, dogs, horses, and a gaggle of particularly nasty-tempered geese. Her humorous writings on barnyard foibles include magazine columns, cowboy and -girl poetry, and her book, The Greenhorn's Guide to the Woolly West. *In this essay, the Country Woman learns to drive the pickup at a snail's pace while the husband throws bales to the cattle. She also learns how to throw the bales when the husband throws his back out again.*

Sometimes fall and Indian summer last all the way to Christmas. More often, the blizzards strike early. A crisp, brilliant, clear sky begins to cloud up. The air grays and thickens, and before long, that thick air congeals into gorgeous snow. The thing about snow is that it's everywhere and all over. Not a twig escapes the cold, white blanket. While you may gaze in awe at the incredible beauty God has wrought over rooftops and fence posts, your man is apt to use the deity's name in vain.

Snow and cold mean the cattle must be fed hay. The very hay you personally helped stack must now be dispensed, a few bales at a time, to the hungry critters.

Your man prefers to feed at daylight (naturally), which means you are required to rise in the middle of the night in order to feed him first. Also, naturally, you are privileged to help with the chores.

Gauge the layers of your outdoor attire by the outdoor temperature. The colder it is, the more sweaters, vests, and warm socks you must don. CAUTION: Avoid squashing yourself too tightly into a many-layered outfit. The circulation can be squeezed from a limb in no time. The pain, when the blood finally begins circulating again, is excruciating.

When feeding in very cold weather, the following toilette procedure is recommended: Circle that long, red, woolen muffler around your neck and up over the hood of your old, red snowsuit. (Dudes from the city call a snowsuit a "snowmobile suit.") Wear your husband's old vest under the snowsuit and his old denim jacket over the outside. As mentioned, the trick is to avoid tourniqueting any part of your body. On your feet, wear the usual high-laced boys' boots over two pairs of thick socks. Slip on large, four-buckle overshoes and buckle the tops over the pant legs. You will look like a displaced, pudgy Eskimo. Try to avoid looking in a mirror or having to use the bathroom while thus outfitted. Lastly, feel your pocket to be sure you have your pocket knife, take up your warm, fleece-lined gloves or mittens, and stagger outdoors. When King-the-Collie rears up to greet you, make sure you are standing near a wall. Being bowled over in the snow on a cold, dark morning is funny only in comic books.

Your man has not been idle. While you have been garbing,* he has been loading the pickup or the tractor's flatbed trailer with bales of hay. Whether you use the pickup or the tractor to feed depends on which pasture you're going to and how deep the snow lies. As a good Country Woman, your job is to drive the vehicle while your man rides behind to throw off the bales. He will designate where he wants you to drive by waving his arms and pointing—similar to the way sheepdogs are directed to maneuver after sheep. You must keep one eye backward to watch your husband's signals** and one eye forward to avoid driving into the irrigation ditches, sinking into a drift, or hitting a

---

*No one knows why it takes a woman three times as long to put on her outdoor gear than it does a man. Try to get a head start dressing so you won't be left having to walk to the haystack again.

** When you can't see the signals due to the height of the load, you must hang one ear out the window and try to interpret the shouts. Attempts to use ESP do not work.

Winter is a time when many tractors and implements sit unused. Like the earth, they lie dormant until spring arrives and a new growing season begins. Daniel Johnson

cow. Never go too fast. A lurching crawl, like a gluey-footed centipede, is the idea.

If you are driving the pickup, your man will yell, "Put it in the hole!" This means you are being ordered to utilize the very lowest gear—called compound.*** The tractor also has an extremely low gear whose location you can't remember. Unless you get really stuck, a tractor can putz along as slowly as you wish even in a higher gear.

Eventually, your man will drop the last bale and signal you to head for home. It is at this point many Country Women lose face. As you shift from compound, do not jerk. Otherwise, you may lose a good man off the tailgate. If you notice he's missing, be sure to stop and pick him up. He'll be a lot madder if he has to walk all the way home.

There are those cruel mornings when it's entirely up to you to throw the bales because your man has put his back out. But he can still drive, although painfully. Ask him to back the outfit smack up against the haystack, then grab a bale hook and climb to the top of the stack. Many Country Men disdain bale hooks as nuisances when loading a hay wagon. Pay no attention. Bale hooks are a boon and a pleasure to the Country Woman. The hook bites satisfyingly deep into the bale. You won't have to wear out fingers and wrench shoulder sockets trying to hang on to those bales by the strings. With a hook, you can drag a bale forward and then lift and heave. Be sure to unhook before you heave, otherwise the hook stays lodged in the bale and follows it down to the haywagon. Worse

*** It doesn't matter what it is called. The important thing is to be aware that when "in the hole," the outfit will inch along over rocks, logs, and up the side of a tree if pointed to it.

128

This painting depicting a winter farmyard scene was very typical of the many farms that dotted the rural landscape in the beginning of the twentieth century

yet, you may still be hanging on to the bale hook handles.*

When the hay load reaches the proper limit,** jump on top and hang on while your man hurtles the vehicle forward to the feed ground. As he puts the outfit into its slow crawl, grab a bale by one of its two strings and give a mighty upward wrench while kneeing the center of the bale at the same time. Theoretically, the bale string will pop off like a rubber band. Then, holding the one length of string, reach down and grab the other string, still around the bale. A quick flip and the bale flops apart and scatters over the edge of the wagon bed. Repeat this with additional bales at regular intervals, first on one side of the outfit, then the other. Each time after dropping a bale, you will be holding two strings, which you then loop over a handy upright pole on the pickup. Later, you will burn the strings.

Unfortunate truth: The theoretically correct method of bale throwing only works some of the time. More often, the blame things fight back. Bale strings refuse to pop off no matter how hard you pull. If that happens, slip off your mittens and hold them in your teeth or, if you don't care for the slobber, stuff them in your back pocket. Dredge out your pocket knife and cut those reluctant bale strings.

Some sort of implement for cutting strings is a must. A tooth from a mower nailed to a stout stick works very well. Hold the tool aloft and bring it sharply down slicing the strings like a guillotine on the head of a wife of Henry the VIII. An old hunting knife is the choice for some. Stick it, point down, in that skinny pocket halfway down the right leg of your snowsuit. When needed, you can whip it out and whack the strings apart. (This particular method has a certain Wild West style to it.)

*At this point, your man's sense of humor asserts itself. He laughs himself silly.
** Try to keep mouth shut when your man comments on the flotsam and jetsam appearance of your load.

Gray silos, full of forage for the winter, tower above the farm and blend into the gray winter skies. Michael Savoie, shutterstock

Round bales are lined up alongside this weathered, red barn. The bales are wrapped with plastic to slow down the spoiling process. Nancy Gill, shutterstock.

> *I prefer winter and fall, when you feel the bone structure in the landscape—the loneliness of it—the dead feeling of winter. Something waits beneath it—the whole story doesn't show.*
> **–Andrew Wyeth**

Sometimes a string will break as you reach for it, scattering hay all over the load but not onto the ground. Or you fall down, lose the whole bale over the edge with strings still tied, and are forced to holler for your man to halt. Then jump down, run back, and break that bale. Tear back to the outfit and haul yourself aboard, which is terribly hard to do in all those clothes, especially as the vehicle always starts forward just before you really arrive.

Finally you finish the job. As your man turns toward home, remain standing on the truck or tractor bed. Firmly clutch anything available. Do not make the mistake of seating yourself on a bare-board floor when returning from the feed ground. To do so will invite painful, long-lasting bruises as your husband guns the vehicle over the terrain, each wheel hitting a different frozen pie.

As soon as you reach the house, dash to the telephone and call the bone doctor. Plead mightily for an immediate appointment to have your husband's

back overhauled, because your own is rapidly fusing into a permanent L-shape.

If you don't create square bales, you and the bank may be the proud owners of equipment that makes those huge round bales. Big machinery sucks up the hay into round pegs the size of a tunnel big enough to drive through if they were hollow. They aren't. To feed these behemoths requires a truck outfitted with a gizmo that has robot arms. Push a button inside the truck cab, and the arms will pluck up a round bale and bring it onto the truck bed. Sort of the way a frog laps up a fly only not so quick.

If you, the True Country Woman, are placed in the position of feeding the cattle on some morning or other, no problem. The bales hit the ground and all you do is clip the strings and push and the bale unrolls like a rug—usually. If it doesn't, then you must jump down and pick a fight with the monster.

Country Woman's Prayer

Consider, Lord, the many days
That livestock I've turned out to graze
All try to hasten my decline
By accident or sly design.

When time to feed the cows again,
Power tools are my best friend.
I load round bales with metal arms,
Cab-controlled, the gadget charms.

Onward now to feed the cows,
One more prayer if the Lord allows,
For when a bale is dropped to ground,
It should unfurl like a rug in town.

It sometimes sticks and scoots along,
Like a dragging log; Lord, something's wrong!
I put 'er in neutral and jump from the truck
To hand-push the bale till it comes unstuck.

Needles of hay stab my hand,
Oh Lord, I've had about all I can stand.
The cows are impatient, they're in my way,
They don't give a durn 'bout people who pray.

But I've three more bales I still must feed,
So, I ask you, Lord, to hear my need.
It's a modest request, it's a simple goal—
Oh, *please* dear Lord, let my bales unroll!

If not for their dark noses and yellow neck tags, these wooly sheep would blend right into the background on this foggy winter day. Sebastian Knight, shutterstock

Thick winter coats keep cattle warm during the winter months. In severe weather, cattle require extra feed to maintain their weight. Joy Brown, shutterstock

Many layers of clothing are a must for anyone who needs to hop on a tractor without a cab during the winter. Chores still need to be accomplished, no matter how cold it is outside. Lori Spankia, shutterstock

Winter snowstorms can be brutal. The snow frozen on this fence is evidence of a recent snowstorm that was accompanied by very strong wind. Egidijus Mika, shutterstock

During the winter, farms may look rather inactive, but inside the doors of the barn and shed is a flurry of activity and life. Liz Van Steenburgh, shutterstock

A farm woman carries a bucket of water from the water pump to her farmhouse during the winter of 1923. Indoor plumbing was something that took a while to make its way into older farmhouses. Extra money usually went straight back into the farm. Wisconsin Historical Society

The thickness of the blanket of snow that has fallen in northwestern Wisconsin during the winter of 1961–1962 is evident in the high sides of the shoveled path to the barn. Courtesy of Kenneth and Shirley Glaser

Warm light glows from inside this barn on a winter morning. Even though the brisk winter winds whip at you as you walk to the barn, as soon as you open the door, you are bathed in the warmth of a barn full of animals. Daniel Johnson

WINTER TALES

By Bob Becker

Bob Becker began writing in 1986 after retiring from a thirty-two-year career with the Wisconsin Department of Natural Resources. His weekly column, "Boot Prints," a mix of outdoor and human interest stories, appeared in several northwest Wisconsin newspapers. Bob has retired from writing columns. He and his wife live in Spooner, Wisconsin.

The following three essays are columns of Bob's that revolve about rural life in the 1930s. The cold northern Wisconsin winters were brutal, but the work still had to be done. His childhood memories emanate with the warm glow of a barn full of cows, Grandma's woodstove, and rosy-cheeked ice skaters.

Winter Mornings

I stand before my dining room window these January mornings and gaze into the darkness of the backyard. Daylight doesn't come until almost eight o'clock these days. I watch the world slowly, gradually, turn from black to white.

I'm sure there are many who hate these late winter mornings. Momma's one of them. She's a brightness-oriented person. Give her a dark day, and she reacts. "This weather's the pits," she'll announce and flip on all the lights in the house.

Not I. I find the gentle softness of semidarkness a soothing respite from the nerve-jangling stimulation of brightness. And I tell her so. "Opposites attract!" she'll come back, shaking her head in dismay.

The backyard is a thing of beauty on these dark, early mornings, especially if the wind isn't blowing. The scene is still and peaceful, serene, as a new page in the book of life waits to be written.

Against a western sky, almost imperceptibly changing to silver, the windbreak of pines and spruces stands black, silhouetted. The woodpile looks husky and solid against the snow, beginning to gray in the gathering light. Like an artist's work done in charcoal, the portrait is slowly painted by Mother Nature's hand, subtle, soft strokes gently caressing the outdoor canvas.

I find my thoughts drifting back to mornings on country farms long ago, times when I peeked through cracks in barn doors and watched cold dawns break on horizons to the east. I suppose I was six, maybe seven; in first grade, maybe second; just beginning to become aware of the workings of the world around me.

My grandfather would begin the day by banging an old wrench on the old-fashioned cast-iron steam radiator in his bedroom. His six sons and three daughters called him "The Boss." The clang of his pounding traveled throughout the house, from bedroom to bedroom, a signal that the time had come to roll out of bed and begin the day's tasks.

Dressing, I'd follow my uncles downstairs to the huge kitchen, the center of all family activity. There, my grandmother would already have the methane-fueled gas lights glowing and a fire crackling in her wood-burning cooking range.

In a huddle in a corner, my uncles slipped into their blue denim barn jackets, pulling four-buckle rubber boots over their work shoes, and as each stepped out the back door, he picked up a shiny stainless-steel milk pail. A couple kerosene lanterns would be lit, and into the cold darkness we marched, the snow crunching and squeaking underfoot, the swinging lanterns casting a moving panorama of pale yellow light and black shadows against the woodpile and trees.

The first stop was the windmill to test the long-handled pump. Was it frozen? Maybe a teakettle of hot water would be retrieved from the kitchen to free its innards.

Snow softens everything on the farm. The peaks and corners of the barn roof aren't as severe. Implements resting for the winter are mysterious forms when they are covered in snow. Daniel Johnson

Then we continued through a wooden barn door, creaking in complaint to the cold, past the pens of young stock and the bull, looking menacing with a big copper ring in his nose, and into the cow barn.

The animals expected us, almost glad to see us. Those lying resting in their straw bedding would rise to their feet; others bellowed their good mornings.

The lanterns were hung from spikes driven into the wooden-beamed rafters, their glow reflecting from the whitewashed ceiling. Taking their three-legged milking stools from wooden pegs on the wall, my uncles would settle beside contented Holsteins and begin their morning milking.

Ping-ping-ping, the streams of milk would echo from the sides of the steel pails held between their knees, gradually changing to a soft squish-squish as the pail began to fill. Silently and mysteriously, a motley bevy of cats, big and small, would sift in from their nests in the haymow, the first rewarded with a well-aimed stream of milk direct from the cow into its opened mouth. The rest fed at a small wooden trough from the first pail of milk.

From cow to cow, my uncles moved; the milk poured into tall milk cans through a large-mouthed strainer with a fresh, clean, cotton filter in its bottom. When the job was done, outside the half-light of the new day would have arrived.

Today I ponder those old times as I stand before my window in the morning darkness. People knew hard work. People didn't have modern conveniences. My hand reaches for the light switch, and in an instant those memories are dimmed, darkened by the brightness that suddenly floods the room.

Ice Skating

Things were quiet, serene, and peaceful out there on the little lake. There I sat, resting on the seat of my ice-fishing sled, jigging for walleyes through a hole in the ice, watching the inert flags of my tip-ups. Dusk was falling.

Cords of firewood that were cut in the fall will help keep the farmhouse warm throughout the long, cold winter. Tyshko V. Vladmir, shutterstock

To the west, behind a band of tall Norway pines, an anemic winter sun was settling. Its last rays casting burnished silver, like that of polished pewter, on the snowless, frozen surface of the lake. Over on the northeast shore, where a summer cottage stands, the slanting sunbeams are reflected in brilliant gold from the dwelling's picture window.

Except for the distant whine of a chainsaw and the raucous crowing of a pair of crows heading for their night's roosting, all was still, almost a classic December "silent night" in northern Wisconsin.

The scene could have been right out of a Currier and Ives painting. Yet inside me, an unsettling instinct stirred, telling me something was amiss.

What? For several fleeting moments the question gnawed at me. And then the answer dawned.

Ice skaters! That's what was missing! A young couple dressed in baggy wools of the 1920s, long red and green scarves trailing behind in the breeze, gliding gracefully over the lake. That's what the picture needed!

Old, long-muted memories began to replay in my brain. Ice skating, you see, was a big thing for my generation of youngsters. This past summer, a brother and I got to reminiscing about our lives as kids back in the late 1930s. "I remember getting a pair of skates for Christmas," Bill said. "I tried them on to make sure they were big enough. And believe me, they were! A couple sizes oversize, so I'd have room to grow into them. Mom made sure of that!"

Experiences like that well typify those times. Money was scarce, people were poor. We youngsters found our recreation in simple ways, like sledding on Deak's Hill or skating on the pond across the road.

139

Winter days are short and often gray and gloomy. Any bit of sunlight that radiates is a blessing to all in the northern snowy climates. Keith Naylor, shutterstock

The little puddle wasn't all that much, maybe a half acre in size, surrounded by big oaks fringing a farm field. We'd gather there after supper. Approach the site and the voices of friends, boys and girls, would grow from a distant murmur in the night air to the excited clamor of country kids having fun.

Kids of all ages and backgrounds were there. The more well-to-do were apparent by the pairs of shoe skates hanging from laces around their necks. The less-well-off were obvious by the old-fashioned clamp skates they carried.

Clamp skates were made to be fastened to the soles of your shoes. With a key, the blades would be tightened in place. In theory, the clamps were supposed to hold. But in reality, they frequently twisted loose, sending frustrated skaters spilling to the ice. Pity the youngster who tore the sole from his shoe in the process for shoes were precious and a scolding was inevitable when the unfortunate one got home.

If the night's cold warranted, wood was gathered, and a fire was built. And in its dim light, makeshift hockey games would organize. There were no store-bought hockey sticks like nowadays, just sturdy crooked sticks cut from bushes and trees. The puck was just a gnarled knot to be batted around until it finally split into pieces. The older, bigger guys, the better and faster skaters, usually played hockey.

The rest of the gang was content to casually skate slowly in circles around the perimeter of the pond, laughing and teasing, with a periodic game of "crack the whip" sending a brave skater sailing at what seemed breathtaking speed across the ice.

For many years now, the little pond has been gone, filled and killed by a housing development that came in the boom following World War II. Yet I know where its waters once stood. And when I visit my home turf, especially in winter, I gaze across the rows of modern homes.

There, marked by a few aged sturdy oaks that still remain, my memory once more paints for me images of youngsters happily skating on moonlit winter evenings. For the fun of it.

This lone Hereford cow gazes across the fence from a field full of cornstalk stubble. Curt Pickens, shutterstock

Farm Breakfasts

Dead-winter mornings are dark, dreary things. I awaken, and outside, the world is black. Daylight arrives slowly in midwinter.

I sip my first cup of coffee, read the morning paper, and still the backyard remains cloaked in gloom. And as breakfast, a batch of Malt-O-Meal, simmers on the kitchen range, my thoughts drift back to mornings long ago, back to my boyhood, back to breakfasts on our farms many years ago.

The bubbling cereal triggers my reminiscing. A hot cereal! Everyone I knew as a boy—my folks, my grandparents, my uncles and aunts—all would say that a bowl of hot cereal, either oatmeal or cornmeal, was the best way for a youngster to start the day—— especially when there was a mile walk through the cold and snow to a country school.

I can hear my grandfather now. "Eat it!" he'd say, as I'd wrinkle my nose at the glue-like oatmeal before me, so thick it'd have to be scraped from the serving spoon. "It's good for you," he'd say. "It'll stick to your

ribs!" Which meant it had staying power. It did, and it is the reason why I hate oatmeal to this day.

I look around our kitchen as I eat, at the array of push-button gadgets that instantaneously respond to our commands: the electric range, the coffeemaker, the toaster, the microwave, and the lights that illuminate the house.

I think about similar dark, dead-winter mornings, back when my grandfather started each day by banging an old wrench on the cast-iron radiator in his bedroom. The clanging carried along the pipes to the upstairs bedrooms where his six sons and three daughters slept. Time to roll out! Cows needed milking, horses needed feeding, the sound said.

By the time the boys, as Grandpa fondly referred to his sons, came marching down the stairs, Grandma would already be busy in her kitchen, building a fire in her wood-burning range. Breakfast had to be prepared for the gang. In an hour or so, the men would be back from their barn chores, and they'd be hungry.

The whiteness of the farmhouse, barn, and landscape is blinding against this bright, blue winter sky. Regina Chayer, shutterstock

Sometimes our fate resembles a fruit tree in winter. Who would think that those branches would turn green again and blossom, but we hope it, we know it.
–Johann Wolfgang von Goethe

Quickly, silently, the menfolk slipped into their barn clothing, heavy denim coats, and four-buckle overshoes. In the entryway, kerosene lanterns would be lighted and shiny milk pails selected. Down the back porch steps into the darkness they slipped, the swinging lanterns casting ghostly shadows with their pale yellow light. Past the big woodpile and the windmill, the snow creaking and crunching under their booted feet. And into the barn they'd disappear, to where the herd of Holsteins and Guernseys patiently waited in their stanchions.

I suppose the milking, the feeding, and the watering of the livestock would take a strong hour of their time. When finished, back to the house they'd drift for breakfast. And what breakfasts they would be! Grandma and her daughters, my aunts, would have been busy, the long oil-cloth-covered table set, the food simmering on her woodstove. Grandpa always sat at the head of the table, the boys along his right, the girls along his left. Grandma at the opposite end—when she had a chance to sit, that is.

From her oven, placed there to keep warm, would come huge platters of eggs fried in bacon grease. You didn't get a choice as to how you'd like yours done. Alongside the eggs were heaping mounds of bacon and pork sausage made from hogs raised on the farm and butchered the previous fall. Then a steaming platter of warmed-over potatoes, also homegrown, deliberately left from supper the night before. Loaves of golden brown bread, baked perhaps the day before in the very same oven, were cut into thick slices, ready for the butter she'd churned or the plum jam she'd canned last summer.

And the best of all! Her buckwheat pancakes! Massive things that covered an entire plate, to be topped with sweet apple butter made from the Yellow Transparents that grew in her orchard. Pancakes made from flour ground at the mill in town, of grain that Grandpa grew in the little patch of buckwheat he planted each spring.

As appetites were staved, spirits improved. Jovial talk rolled around the table. Grandpa would get in his licks as to what he expected his crew to accomplish that day. Things like pulling a crosscut saw in the woods cutting firewood or fanning seed oats in the granary for spring planting.

I look back at those long-ago breakfasts with mixed feelings. Certainly, they were wonderful family times. Yet, I find myself amazed at how those old-timers did it, especially my grandmother. Seven days a week, most of her life, she made those breakfasts. And when we'd get up from her table to resume our days, it'd still be dark outside.

Two rays of sunshine break through to shine upon this snow-covered field. Socrates, shutterstock

Just because this tractor is covered in a dusting of snow doesn't mean that work doesn't need to be completed during the winter months. Dust off the seat and the tractor is ready to roll. Mark Yuill, shutterstock

Gloomy winter days can be hard to get through, but thoughts of melting snow and the warm spring winds help many survive the long winter season. Richard A. McGuirk, shutterstock

When you live in Texas, every single time you see snow, it's magical.
–Pamela Ribon, Why Girls Are Weird

Frost covers the thin, bare branches of the trees in the distance. This type of day is perfect for taking the snowmobile for a spin around the back forty. Laitr Keiows, shutterstock

The fluffy flakes on snow-covered wheat provide a stark contrast against the bright, blue winter sky. Romeo Koitmae, shutterstock

The frozen pond in the distance is the perfect place to glide around on ice skates. Andrew F. Kazmierski, shutterstock

Snow has the ability to make something as simple as a fence look beautiful and artistic. Daniel Johnson

CHRISTMAS KALEIDOSCOPE

By Ben Logan

Ben Logan traveled as a merchant seaman, and worked many years as a novelist, producer, writer of films and television, and lecturer while living forty miles north of New York City. Yet his roots remained in the southwestern Driftless area of Wisconsin. He returned to his childhood farm "Seldom Seen" in the mid-1980s and has lived there ever since. His book The Land Remembers: The Story of a Farm and Its People *was published in 1975 and is now in its eighth edition.*

"Christmas Kaleidoscope" is an essay from Ben's Christmas Remembered *collection of stories and reflects how reminiscing is like looking through a kaleidoscope. With each spin of the kaleidoscope is another Christmas memory of the past, full of bright jewel tones and crisp details that will forever be ingrained into the recesses of the mind.*

I was hillborn, brought into life in southwestern Wisconsin's rough and beautiful land. There I learned as a child, without knowing I was learning, that the year has five seasons, not four.

Christmas was the fifth season. It reached out to us on our ridge-top farm, interrupting those tag end days when wind howled around the eaves, and our spirits were as shriveled as the few stubborn apples still clinging to the Wolf River tree. In years of depression or plenty, happy times or sad times, land sparkling with white or laying bare and gray, the season of Christmas found us, bringing so much, seeming to ask so little in return. Each year I longed for its coming, then joined it and did not want it ever to end.

Even when I was very young, Christmas was already a time of memory. It reached back beyond my birth. I could see earlier Christmases in the way Mother hung a favorite, faded ornament on the tree, the way Father's face softened when he sang a Christmas carol in Norwegian, and in stories told by my three older brothers.

Reach back into all the Christmases of these early years and what do I find? It is all bits and pieces, everything one at a time. I am looking again into my first kaleidoscope, a Christmas present identical to that of my brother, Lee, but I could not and do not believe his had images half as fabulous as mine.

A kaleidoscope, of course, is an instrument of magic. Shake it! Look into it! Random fragments move into patterns, some just color and beauty, others subtle beginnings of something almost familiar. Then the mind, which is also an instrument of magic, can seize those beginnings, make them grow, and connect them into a whole, the way one can assemble the pieces of a puzzle.

Shake the kaleidoscope of memory, close my eyes, and it begins to happen. Only then, going back beyond thought, beyond too neatly arranged chronologies of time and taken-for-granted rituals that hide the truth, do I find glimpses of what made it Christmas.

Shake the kaleidoscope. I am scratching through frost on my bedroom window to find if the outside world looks different on Christmas morning. I find a lifeless-looking stillness, the white curve of a hilltop field like the outline of a sleeping miniature planet, and beyond it the woods where brown leaves cling to the white oaks. It is all silent and frozen, and summer will never come again. As though to argue with me and say the land is never still and lifeless, there is movement. A rust brown color that seems bright as a summer flower is moving along the curve of the hilltop field—a red fox, almost strutting as though it knows I am watching.

Close my eyes again. I am in the cellar, surrounded by smells from the earth, the orange light of my lantern barely holding back the watching, cobwebbed darkness. Whistling bravely, I snatch potatoes from the big bin and dig beets and carrots from the shelves. Making several trips up the steep stairs, escaping the

Father and child take a break from decorating the tree to gaze longingly at the wonderful bird Mother is preparing for Christmas dinner. Mother is opening her sturdy International Harvester chest freezer, which is full of food grown and raised on the farm. This holiday vision appeared in the 1952 International Harvester calendar.

pursuing darkness just in time, I pile my treasures on the pantry floor and slam shut the trapdoor. Mother, seeing that, gives me a hug and smiles at the gathered bounty, her mind already putting it together into Christmas dinner.

Shake the kaleidoscope. A bright red cardinal is on a bough of the white pine beyond the porch, new-fallen snow on the green behind it. It sits as though waiting to be noticed, because this is Christmas Day, and it can decorate a tree as well as we can. I move closer. The cardinal flits away, bringing down a flurry

of white flakes that glitter and change color, red and blue and yellow, as they fall through the sunlight.

Then it is a bleak, soggy day, and we are taking the tobacco down from the shed, even if it is Christmas, handing the fog-softened plants that are speared onto laths to someone below, who hands them to someone farther below, who piles them. Chilled to the bone, we go back to a house filled with cooking smells, and we huddle around the stove. Pinpoints of orange flame and tiny puffs of smoke escape where sheets of black metal join, the burning

BEST CHRISTMAS WISH

CHRISTMAS GREETINGS

CHRISTMAS HAPPINESS BE YOURS

If we had no winter, the spring would not be so pleasant; if we did not sometimes taste of adversity, prosperity would not be so welcome.
–Anne Bradstreet

Idyllic winter scenes are depicted on these vintage postcards from the early 1900s.

151

The sun sets on an old tree not far from the town of Fall Creek, Wisconsin. Lee Klancher

Opposite:
Snow sparkles in front of this old shed in central Wisconsin. Lee Klancher

wood giving us the closest thing to sun we have seen for days.

Shake the kaleidoscope. One of my brothers is saying, as one of them will say every year, "Remember the time the dog knocked the Christmas tree down?" Had they thought about it, surely my brothers would have said that I was too small then to "know anything about anything." That does not matter. The kaleidoscope tells me I am part of the story. I can see a brown and white dog peering out from beneath the tree, a string of white popcorn in his mouth. I can see the dog being untangled from the strings. I can see my mother rescuing an ornament, cradling it a moment in her hands. I can hear the laughter and almost surely there is a discussion (called arguing when parents are present) about who cut the crossboards at the bottom of the tree too short, or would it have happened anyway because someone mixed up the bowls and put already buttered popcorn on the string? Then the tree is straight again and Mother lights the candles, first putting the dog outside, of course, and Father, never trusting the combination of pine needles and candle flames, stands by with a bucket of water.

Shake the kaleidoscope again. My brothers and I are hurtling down the hillside on our sleds, coasting on past the steaming, open water of the spring, all the way to the creek. Two neighbor boys join us and we take long runs along the creek bank, then step onto the ice and slide as far as we can go, teetering and yelling, trying not to fall and almost always falling. Our legs tangled up with one another, and too weak from laughing to get up, we sprawl with our heads on the ice, hearing the creek water bubbling its way downstream to the rivers and the sea. And we argue

This farmhouse is located in New Jersey's Monmouth Battlefield State Park. The revolutionary battle took place on June 28, 1778, and the park preserves the eighteenth-century landscape of the area. Andrew F. Kazmierski, shutterstock

Opposite:
Afternoon sun reflects off the grain bins on a winter day. These bins are full of grain to last throughout the year until the next harvest in the fall. Jason Kasmuovic, shutterstock

about whether or not the creek water will ever return as rain.

"But how would you know it's the same water?"

"How long does it take?"

"Why isn't it salty, if it comes back from the sea?" That would be the voice of my skeptical brother, Junior.

Voices still linking us in the dusk, the four of us and the two neighbor boys climb our separate hillsides toward home, sleds rattling behind us, weighing a thousand pounds, and we go on yelling back and forth until there is nothing left but echoes. Then we are back in the warm house, starving and eating Christmas dinner all over again.

Look back again. I am in the Lewis Store in Gays Mills. Father searches for a Christmas present for Mother, seeming awkward in that section of the store where all the other shoppers are women. He holds up a rose-colored comforter and looks at me and asks, "What do you think?"

"It's beautiful," I say, and his face has the broadest smile I have ever seen there. At home I clutch the comforter close to me, feeling its warmth, as I steal silently into the house while Father distracts Mother in the kitchen. I force the resisting bulk into a cardboard box and hide it under my bed, knowing I will have to watch carefully and move it at least once before Christmas. Mother is a determined sweeper and enemy of winter dust. Finally, it is Christmas morning. She holds the comforter against her, tears in her eyes, cheeks matching the

rose of the cloth, and she goes to Father and gives him a hug.

Memory of the comforter does not end there. It became a special part of our lives, its color and warmth covering each of us in turn when we were ill and slept on the dining room couch. There, close to the heating stove and the open door to Father and Mother's bedroom. I can feel the comforter being pulled up close as Mother "tucks me in," then blows out the kerosene lamp, the charring wick leaving a momentary glow in the room.

Shake the kaleidoscope. I see the orange, winking light of kerosene lanterns moving across the fields in early evening darkness, and soon the house is warmed with neighbors. There is play, laughter, and music, the smell of popcorn, cocoa, and coffee. Then something in Christmas brings back the old tales, my own father sailing from Norway in 1898, new settlers coming in, others moving on to places greener, freer, emptier, or whatever it is that always lies to the west.

A neighbor man, the one with a mournful face, says something about "the lost frontier." Then there is talk about what is gone—passenger pigeons, bears, elk, wolves, the Indians, land virgin and unspoiled, streams running clear after rains. There is even a buffalo. Another man says he read somewhere that the last one in Wisconsin was killed in 1832.

The man with the mournful face says, "Lot of things we could have done better."

There is a silence after the man's words. I can feel a sadness in the room. I expect it to be Mother who will find a way to rescue Christmas from this sudden somberness. But it is Father. He sits nodding, staring straight ahead. He did that sometimes in the middle of a conversation. I always thought he was arranging his Norwegian thoughts into his careful English. "Well," he says. "I think the question is not did we always do the best we could have. The question is do we learn anything as we go along, then do better next time."

Mother pours more coffee and cocoa. The talk goes back to lighter things, stories that begin with "Remember the time" and bring us back to laughter and the familiar feel of Christmas.

Then the winking lanterns take the neighbors back across the snow-covered fields to home, the voices and the pungent smell of corncob pipe smoke still floating through the house.

The years, looked at through the kaleidoscope, are not neatly organized. It is not time, but ideas and feelings that link us together and give continuity to our lives.

Suddenly, it is another Christmas season, one without snow, and I am with Father. The two of us walk out across one of the fields. He is telling me about his childhood in Norway, and I can see him running with his brothers along a path that is close to the cold North Sea. His face is open and smiling, his sternness put aside for Christmas along with worries

about a new growing season that may be filled with drought or insects or hail or weather too hot for oats and too cold for corn. The northwest wind tears at our coats. In the plowed field under our feet, puffs of soil are picked up and are drifting off like black snow. Father sees that happening and frowns. I can almost hear him thinking, "It took a hundred years to make an inch of that topsoil." I hold my breath, afraid I will send him too soon back into the non-Christmas world. "Have to do that different another year," is all he says. He smiles and puts his hand on my shoulder. We turn and walk, side by side like two adults, into the cutting wind, back toward the farmhouse, smoke from the chimneys telling us of the warmth that waits for us there.

Go on shaking the kaleidoscope, and the images come faster and faster. Strings of red cranberries on the tree. Sundogs in the west. A snowy owl sitting in the oak we call the section tree. Father quietly singing a Norwegian song as he reads for the third, fourth, or fifth time a letter from his mother. The incredible red of a Delicious apple. The ripping sound of a Hubbard squash opening ahead of the knife. Bread dough, filled with living yeast, rising above the sides of the bowl. Bittersweet berries encased in ice. Teakettle lifting its lid up and down, sending puffs of steam out the spout. A pan of hot fudge melting a hole down into crusted snow. Steam from the body heat of the cattle coming out around the edge of the barn door and the stored smell of summer in the

The quiet sound of a gentle snowfall is part of the muted, winter soundtrack. Daniel Johnson

Opposite:
Many farmers would have loved for Santa to bring a new Deere planter for the new year. This vintage advertisement was for the new No. 9 planter offered by the Deere & Mansur Co.

haymow. A single red leaf, driven from hiding by wind, blowing along the top of the snow. A tinseled star at the top of the tree, always speaking of ancient times and three wise men, reminding me of Father as a young sailor on the open sea, guided home by stars, lighthouses, and now, by Mother's lamp in the kitchen window.

They are unending, those bits and pieces of childhood years, so close to me, I can almost reach out and touch the heart of Christmas, so full of people I have loved, so linked with knowing I am part of the living land, so filled with who and what I am.

> *There is nothing in the world more beautiful than the forest clothed to its very hollows in snow. It is the still ecstasy of nature, wherein every spray, every blade of grass, every spire of reed, every intricacy of twig, is clad with radiance.*
> **–William Sharp**

I let the images come again.

I am seeing Mother at the zinc-topped kitchen table planning our Christmas, bringing all of herself back from whatever dreams sometimes took her off along in her mind to other places, finding in this fifth season of the year whatever it was she searched for.

I see myself and my brothers, some of our bickering stilled at Christmas, playing together, needing each other, taste buds of the mind all turned on, and we are filled with a sense of newness and belonging that carries us on past Three Kings Days into the faithful seasons of another year.

Delicate footprints from animals and birds mar the pristine surface of freshy fallen snow. Dhoxax, shutterstock